The Garden
Maker's Manual

The Garden Maker's Manual

Rosemary Alexander
& Richard Sneesby

The English Gardening School

TIMBER PRESS
Portland, Oregon

This book was conceived, edited, designed and packaged for the publisher by
Pippa Rubinstein and Judith Robertson, R & R Publishing.

First published in North America in 2005 by
Timber Press, Inc.
The Haseltine Building
133 S.W. Second Avenue, Suite 450
Portland, Oregon 97204-3527, USA
www.timberpress.com

Cataloging-in-Publication Data
A catalog record for this book is available from the Library of Congress.

ISBN 0-88192-704-X

Printed and bound in China

CONTENTS

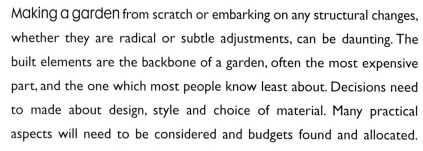

INTRODUCTION

Many different elements have been conbined in this small urban garden. Unity of design style, colour and geometry creates a space which is functional, diverse, relaxing and stimulating.

Making a garden from scratch or embarking on any structural changes, whether they are radical or subtle adjustments, can be daunting. The built elements are the backbone of a garden, often the most expensive part, and the one which most people know least about. Decisions need to made about design, style and choice of material. Many practical aspects will need to be considered and budgets found and allocated.

Some larger additions or alterations may require permission; many will affect neighbours and some might even have a significant impact upon surrounding areas. Making and changing gardens involves a process that may continue over several years as the garden evolves and matures.

Often built elements are unnecessary. Many materials are extraordinarily damaging to the environment, comparatively short-lived in design terms, and leave a legacy of waste and decay when finished with. Always question the use of a material that involves a lot of extraction and energy in its production, over a renewable one. Ask yourself whether, just because 'that's the way it's always been done', it remains the best way today. Technology advances and our understanding of global resources has forced manufacturers to change and improve their attitude towards the environment. Destroying a beautiful natural environment in order to 'improve' a man-made garden is as undesirable as it is irresponsible.

It is important not be afraid to experiment with design. But remember that it is no accident that, throughout the world and throughout history, built garden structures tend to look similar. This is because the laws of physics, and especially the relationship between the strength of materials and their ability to support their own weight, limit their size and shape. It will always be worth referring to existing examples, both new and traditional, before trying something wholly new. It is not always possible to design elements on appearance alone, although technological advances in structural engineering and in new materials have meant that nowadays many seemingly bizarre structures are possible.

Right **Garden** structures, walls and surfaces provide an opportunity to add broad splashes of colour to gardens.

This book has been written to help homeowners and professionals involve themselves in a decision-making process. Each chapter is organized into three sections. The first covers matters of design and appearance, including layout and the design context, selection of materials and a range of design options, and illustrates some successful design precedents. The second section, called 'Practicalities' explains how to achieve many of the results described in the design section, and includes many construction principles and rules of thumb. The third section is a photographic directory of further ideas designed to help you formulate your own. At the end of the book, a final chapter on 'Materials' gives practical advice and technical information. Finally a 'Sources' section provides contacts for all manner of materials and resources.

It is impossible to try to predict every conceivable eventuality that readers of this book will encounter. It is not a case of choosing, from the book a quick design solution. In fact, very few standard details are offered because there is no such thing as a standard solution. The earth is infinitely variable and a solution that may be appropriate in one situation may be wholly inappropriate somewhere else, even within the same garden. Try to gather a full understanding of your garden and decide which is the most suitable set of options. As each chapter includes a list of 'key design questions', this might form a simple checklist to help you in the early stages of creating a design. For most people, this should be the starting point.

Whilst the book divides aspects of landscaping the garden into nine distinct elements, with chapters on each, all gardens will be made from at least two, and sometimes all nine of these elements. Photographs and illustrations show the relationships and connections between the elements, which – in combination with the vital element of planting – help turn ideas into visual compositions: useable, enjoyable and meaningful places which will stand the test of time.

Inevitably, some situations will not be described. In this case, try to adapt the advice to your own situation, but if in any doubt, consult a professional garden designer, landscape architect, garden contractor, engineer or a good builder. Know your limitations: it is better to invest in professional and candid advice than make expensive and perhaps dangerous mistakes.

Before embarking upon any changes, gather as much information about the garden as you possibly can, including plans, photos, legal documents and any maps, old pictures, surveys and drawings showing the location of underground services. Collect images of other gardens you like and that inspire you, including samples of materials and colours as well as things that you really dislike – all of which will help when discussing ideas with design professionals. When making design decisions, ask yourself some of the key design questions listed and be absolutely sure that, from the vast range of possible options (especially those plucked from

High-quality traditional garden architecture is timeless and can be used in many different settings worldwide.

magazines, books and television), you have selected the most appropriate to your situation. Make sure you know how all members of the family or community, especially children, the elderly and those with mobility problems will use the space. Consider how the built elements will work with your favourite plants. Be realistic about money and remember that most projects do go over budget. So do not underestimate the cost of removing existing materials and bear in mind that employed labour will account for at least two-thirds of your budget. Consider life span. How long does the element have to last and how much maintenance will be required to keep it looking good and performing well?

Finally, always remember that gardens are there to be enjoyed. If something does not work, then change it.

Structures can be added to gardens to frame views, provide enclosure and to make intimate spaces suitable for gathering, relaxing and entertaining.

1

PATHS & PAVING

Paths & paving are two vital elements necessary in almost every garden and, because they are highly visible features, it is essential that you explore their design and construction potential before buying materials and starting to build. The earth's surface can be vulnerable and fragile, especially where human beings, animals and vehicles constantly put pressure on it. The natural processes of precipitation – water, wind and frost – can dramatically erode it. Paths and paving serve a double purpose, protecting the earth's surface, while at the same time making it comfortable and pleasant to use.

Paths are the arteries of the garden – leading you from one area to another and around bends and corners. A well considered path system, punctuated with focal points and resting places, could carry you round several acres without your making any conscious effort or even noticing the distance that you have travelled. Paths also form the lines of communication between house and garden, often shaping a major part of the layout by indicating and underlining the structure and providing a framework from which areas, spaces and features can be accessed. Paths can be manipulated in their width, thickness, colour, texture, direction, shape and flow. Bold lines will help to reinforce a strong, confident design, while gentle, understated paths may be appropriate in a more informal or naturalistic garden.

Paving can provide the essential link between indoors and outdoors, or a level platform for relaxing, viewing or stepping off to enjoy the rest of your garden. Paved areas may also be important for access to maintenance areas or as hardstanding for storing equipment.

Both paths and paving may combine with bridges, boardwalks or stepping stones – they can be straight, geometric and formal, perhaps slicing through the underlying

TYPICAL COMPONENTS OF A RIGID AND FLEXIBLE PATH

Above left
Interspersed with moss, these random stepping stones direct the eye to the pathway between the grass banks.

Above right
Harmonizing in colour and texture, mellow toned brick and cobbled paths converge towards a seat which forms a a focal point.

shape of the land or hugging the curves of a sloping garden where they can help to define the organic shape. Paths can offer smoother textures, lighter colours and cooler surfaces (ideal in hotter climates); compact and stable materials for vehicles, softer (and inedible) materials for young children; easier surfaces for wheelchairs, children's prams and strollers; noisy surfaces to announce arrival and uncomfortable surfaces in areas close to danger or where you wish to discourage use.

Both relaxation and active use, as well as children's needs for bicycling or skate boarding, need to be considered and doors and gates opening across paths should be avoided. Gradients must also be suitable for the ability of users. Larger paved areas for tables and chairs should be flat and stable enough to prevent penetration of table and chair legs.

Choosing materials

For centuries designers and builders have selected materials based upon local resources. They will have used clay bricks in an area where clay prevails, or local stone where this occurs naturally. Today materials suitable for paving come from all over the world, at a surprisingly low cost and provide us with a vast array of colours, textures, shapes and sizes; the range increasing all the time as technology develops and as manufacturing, extraction and transport becomes more efficient. New materials, and alternative ways of using more traditional ones, are being tested all the time, some with great success, while others, although technically sound, just look contrived. Most people, however, choose materials that have stood the test of time, but may also look for new ways of using them.

Choose materials suited both to the garden layout and your budget. Costly projects may need materials that look expensive but are not necessarily so. Contemporary designs may allow new and innovative ways of using and detailing materials. Less formality and control may be more suitable in country areas or where the approach is naturalistic or ecological. From the outset, you should bear in mind the environmental implications of your selection. Cheap materials, especially imported ones, often have hidden environmental consequences for their country of origin.

Although the appearance of the surface is likely to govern your decision, the paving must also be practical, reinforcing the ground beneath, while withstanding the load and wear it will receive. For example, bark is attractive in informal areas, but will need replacing every couple of years. Ceramic glazed tiles can look effective, but may be dangerous when wet and frozen. Your chosen surface must be durable and maintain its strength and integrity through its design life. It must also allow water to drain away quickly to ensure that it remains safe and useable.

Ideally the garden design should be in sympathy with the locality, so take a lead from your surroundings. What are the buildings made from? What colour are walls and surfaces? What colour is the soil or local rock? You may not want to use the same material, but should consider complementary colour, tone, texture and shade.

Choose materials that fit in with your overall design intentions, design style or theme. Clean minimalist lines might suggest using a single material where the shades and tones may derive from how the material is detailed or how it is affected by cast or reflected light. Local building traditions and skills may well be important and you may wish to get craftsmen to combine materials to make intricate patterns or decorative motifs.

A change of direction is indicated by the locations of joints in this poured (in situ) concrete path. The hard edges are softened with groundcover planting.

By studying the wider design context, a clear architectural style may emerge. Choose materials that unify house and garden by being similar or complementary in appearance and style.

Instead of resorting to inert materials, it is sometimes wiser to leave the existing surface in place, or to use grass paths. A grass walk through the centre of two areas of planting can provide an informal link between path and planting. Where the climate and situation allows it to flourish, grass is a wonderfully cool surface, but may not stand up to constant use, such as under a seat or child's swing, where the turf will become unsightly and possibly dangerous when wet. Existing soil and rock surfaces may also be suitable without any need for alteration.

Design principles

Because paths are linear elements within the garden, they can serve to guide and control how the garden is used; to give access to views, focal points and places for gathering and relaxation. Paths can be given a hierarchy by width, with the wider ones having the status of a main route, whilst narrower paths and different surfaces might indicate that they are for more occasional use. Paths should always be located for a reason. In particular, avoid creating junctions where people might be tempted to cut the corner and trample plants or wear away grass edges.

Various visual devices can be used to make the path seem longer, shorter, narrower or wider. For instance, bringing the edges closer together as the path disappears into the distance will make it appear longer; placing a focal point, large or small, at the end of a path will also accentuate its length.

Conversely, placing a group of small objects in the immediate foreground will make the path seem wider or shorter. Layouts visualized on paper will always foreshorten on the ground. A path that allows two or more people to walk side-by-side while chatting encourages a more enjoyable, gentle saunter, whereas a narrow path, with room for only one at a time, tends to hurry people along. A wide area with a seat

Bricks should be laid to reinforce the direction of flow along a path. Note the direction changes on the secondary route to the left.

Centred on a line with the French windows, the two parallel rows of smooth paving stones serve to break up this wide cobbled path, making walking easier.

Appears longer   Appears shorter

By varying the direction of joints between units, paths can be made to appear longer or shorter and wider.

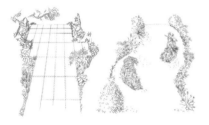

Choose materials that suit the overall pattern: rectangular units for geometric shapes, gravel or concrete for freeforms.

invites you to linger. A path curving around the edge of a space will create a totally different experience from one that cuts through the middle.

Adding focal points or incidents will give drama or interest to your paths: a glimpse of a bench or an urn can encourage you to walk to it; at the arrival point there may be a choice of direction with another intriguing view or object that you wish to explore, so tempting you forward along the path without you really noticing.

Paths can be a series of parallel lines that divide the space up into blocks. Bold geometric shapes with strong lateral lines that the eye can follow as you progress through the garden give a sense of great control and order. Horizontal patterning accentuated by planting allows the eye to move from side to side. Key plants located diagonally along a path will carry the eye forward. Where paths are narrow, perhaps to go through an arch or between planting, they can create a sense of anticipation until they widen out again.

People have a tendency to avoid walking in straight lines and long straight paths can be uncomfortable. Straight lines drawn on maps and plans may become paths that are steep and difficult to negotiate when translated on to sloping ground. Paths that curve and snake their way through a garden can be more responsive to the site as well as generally being more comfortable. On sloping and undulating ground, paths can traverse across slopes rather than over them, the path following the contours or slowly rising up the slope as it curves around. Curved paths of irregular width can be

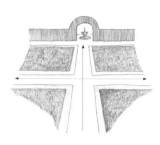

Choice of path layout and geometry may well be the most important design decision you make, and can define a whole area of the garden.

Centred on a Lutyens-style seat, and set for ease of mowing at a slightly higher level than the paving stones, these grass inserts break up the width of the path.

very artistic especially if accentuated with more than one material. If plants are taken through paving, try to make them appear as if the route of the path has been caused by avoiding existing plants.

Avoid creating 'stepping stone' paths across grass, as they always result in an awkward, self-conscious effect and make the turf less easy to mow.

Path widths are largely determined by the following:

- status of the route
- number of people and vehicles that will use them (wheelbarrows, etc),
- available ground space
- scale and proportions of the garden
- cost of construction
- choice of surface material and the suitability of the ground
- main routes will also include access routes, for example from house to garage, or to fuel stores in winter months

Generally paths of 1.0–1.2m(3ft6in–4ft) are wide enough for generous use in a garden situation, with up to 1.5m(5ft) being preferable for two people walking side-by-side. The minimum path width for a secondary path is around 900mm(3ft), although narrower paths, through planting beds or vegetable plots, for example, are possible. So that unnecessary cutting is avoided, the detailed dimensions of paths made from unit materials will be determined by the size of the units themselves. Make sure that there is sufficient turning room for any maintenance equipment, such as lawnmowers or ride-on tractors.

Larger paved surfaces: terraces and patios

Larger areas of paving, concentrated into flat terraces or patios, provide a useful and durable surface for entertaining and activities that would otherwise wear away unprotected ground. Their overall shape will emerge from general design decisions and the ability to achieve it with sourced materials that fall within your budget. Simple squares and rectangles are easy to construct from rectilinear units supplied as slabs, bricks and paving blocks. Curved, circular and more organic shapes may be extremely difficult to construct from readily available building units, but will be simple to make from more fluid construction materials, such as gravel and *in situ* or poured concrete.

The varied sizes of stone slabs used for this meandering path allow planting to encroach informally over the edge and avoid the need for clear definition.

Carefully located paths that curve around site features, reinforce the relationship between circulation routes and design composition.

Striking architecture might suggest patterns and layout for paving.

A smooth transition between interior and exterior is achieved by using the same paving stones throughout, their light colour and uniform size contrasting with dark stone walling.

Larger areas for outdoor living should be considered as flat, although in practice they should slope slightly for drainage. This might mean including a low wall along some edges in order to raise the level, and steps or ramps to return it to surrounding ground level.

Existing or proposed buildings or structures might suggest shapes and patterns, perhaps associated with the rhythm of doors, windows or framing elements. Landform and availability of level ground might dictate the outer limits of the paving. Unlike most paths, these larger areas provide an occasion for patterns with straight lines, right angles, geometric shapes and smooth surfaces to indicate formality, while loose, natural curves and rough or textured finishes tend to be informal.

Orientation of the paved area will also be important. What can you see from the paving? Where are the good views? Where are the sunny spots? There is little point in locating one of the main features of the garden in a miserable shady place with a poor view, just because it is close to the house, when a more pleasant location might be just a small distance away.

These areas must also be functional. How many people will use the space? Will more space be required for parties and gatherings? If space allows, a minimum of 4m(13ft) in any one direction should provide a useful and adaptable area. Sufficient room is needed for pushing back chairs after a meal (approximately 1.5m[5ft]), for moving between sun loungers, perhaps beside a swimming pool, or for pushing a loaded wheelbarrow or trolley. If the use of chairs and tables is planned, a smooth solid surface will prevent them rocking, but textured finishes will be less slippery.

Finally, consideration must be given to the relationship between indoors and outdoors. The use of the same surface material on either side of a glass door can create an exciting continuity and transition so long as the material is durable outdoors. Contrasting materials can also be used to good effect but be careful not to muddle styles, colours, textures and quality of finish.

Vehicle drives and parking areas

Most of the general principles of paths and paved areas will also apply to vehicle access driveways and parking areas. Construction will need to be deeper and stronger, edges and drainage will need to be carefully detailed, and consideration given to their appearance, as they will usually be most visible from public areas where they can make a significant contribution to the locality. Driveways may also be required occasionally for loading and unloading, house removals or emergency access and so need to be suitable for larger vehicles, particularly if the house some way from a road. Generally, cars require a single drive width of 3m(9ft9in), and, if two vehicles are to pass, 6m(19ft6in) is required. Allow space for access to side doors, especially to unload children and larger objects from rear seats. Provide space around parking areas for organizing luggage and for storing trailers, boats, caravans, etc. If a site has limited access, local provisions may require as much as 6m(20ft) to accommodate emergency services. A turning area would make life much easier for all vehicles although it would take up a lot of space.

Choice of surface material

The selection of the surface material or materials will have the most significant impact upon the overall appearance of the path or paved area. Working with colour, pattern, texture and motif derived from the various materials and the way in which they are combined or jointed together gives an almost infinite range of possibilities. Given that there is such a vast choice, a little time spent choosing the appropriate material will pay dividends in the long run.

Larger rectilinear units, such as slabs or flags, will cover ground quickly and may lead to rectilinear patterns. However, avoid choosing rectilinear units for curved and complex patterns where they would need cutting. Smaller units and granular materials would be a better choice in this situation. Generally unit paving allows easier access to underground services, to the sub-grade, sub-base and base layers for maintenance purposes, as units can be lifted and replaced with little or no evidence that a repair has been carried out. They are also easy to handle, involve little use of large machinery and can be used in areas where access is limited; best of all, they are also usually ready for use immediately after laying.

Choose a material that will not involve unnecessarily heavy labour costs. A lot of cutting could double the cost of the paving, and laying small units for complex patterns will take time. Appearance, wearing strength and the necessary underlying base courses will all affect the cost or estimate, so it is crucial to use an appropriate material which will not require unnecessary labour. Gravel can create an almost instant effect, is less expensive, and can be poured into almost any shape, but does not provide a stable surface for chairs and tables and can be a nuisance when carried elsewhere on shoes.

Most materials can be used in a flexible construction system (see Practicalities on page 26), but some thin, small and more fragile materials must be mortared on to a solid concrete slab which may involve excavation and more expensive construction, even though the surface materials may themselves be inexpensive.

Colour and tone   From a huge and bewildering range of hard surfacing materials, it is difficult to decide on the most suitable for any particular job. Before committing to a particular material, look at it in both full sun and on a dull day, and then try wetting the material to see how the colour changes. Do not base your decision on looking at one slab, one brick, or a small bag of gravel. Try to see the material used *en masse* so that you can visualize how it will work as a path or larger paved area.

A wide range of colours is available, usually based on earthy tones derived from natural materials. Other more intense colours, made from pigmented and 'white' cement, mastic binders, ceramics and painted finishes, are also available. Variety of textures is also extensive mainly based upon the material selected and method of

Filling the cracks with moss (thereby avoiding the need for cement or some other inert material), not only enhances the textures and varied colours of this stone paving, but also forms a sinuous pattern.

finishing. If slip resistance is important, opt for a textured surface, but bear in mind that weathering, algae growth and decay can all affect the surface of some materials.

Surface patterns and appearance Many designers and homeowners start by producing patterns for areas of paving on plan drawings. This basic design intention will have an important influence upon the choice of materials. Of course, many things are possible with the range of materials available, but to ease the construction and to minimize cost some basic rules should be applied.

Paths of embedded cobblestones converge between formal planting. Within the cobblestone paving, and around the circular central feature, terracotta bricks are used to create a central 'sunburst' effect.

Mixing material to create patterns Try to use materials of similar thickness so that the construction of base courses and bedding layers can be set to a fairly uniform level before surface materials are put into position. Remember that several different small, irregular units may not fit together tightly and so may move unless jointed together with a stable material, such as mortar, that will be very visible at the surface. Rectangular and square units can make attractive rectilinear patterns that should be based upon multiples of whole units to avoid cutting.

Drainage falls and changes in level, such as access ramps, may look convincing on flat drawings, but when built will almost always involve careful cutting of units to achieve the level change option. This means that flat slabs cannot be bent over the

Slowing do...
approac...
Japanes...
the width...
of this ra...
path...
importa...

subtle slopes required for surface drainage. They will need to be cut and the joints will register at the surface as an unintentional pattern (see below).

Joints Joints between paving units will appear as obvious lines on the ground, so will need to be thought about carefully at the design stage. There are plenty of examples of successful paving where patterns, direction and flow are based entirely upon the design of the ...self receding into the background. In rigid paving systems, ...dation, movement joints in the base slab will need to carry ...d will, therefore, register as a significant part of the pattern.

...e basic rules in mixing materials

...s based upon loose and bound aggregates do not require joints. ...ay be manufactured or cut with flush joints which are barely ...en viewed from a distance.

...match the colour of jointing material exactly, especially when ...ed material, such as clay bricks and natural ...e colour of the joints will need to be very ...en.

 ...the colour of joints can have a dramatic effect on paving patterns.

 Changing the size and shape of joints can also have a dramatic effect.

 Brushing sand or a sand/soil mixture into joints will encourage crevice plants (and weeds!).

Edges to paths and paved areas

Most paths and paved areas require edges which, in the case of paths, may be the most important visual element. Edges may be required in order to:

Prevent lateral spread of granular and flexible paving materials in all but the most rural of situations.

Collect water and channel it into collection points, as all paved surfaces must slope to allow drainage water to be shed to the

Crazy paving updated. Repeated on the low retaining wall, ceramic tiles bring light and texture to the floorscape leading to this highly decorative arch.

sides. So edges should stand proud of the surface, gather water and guide it away into collection points such as gulleys, channels or ditches.

Connect different surfaces and mark boundaries, for example, where a side path meets a main route, or where a maintenance route joins a pedestrian path. Also two surfaces of differing construction or similar construction, but with different materials, may need an edge between them.

Ease maintenance operations, where soft surfaces (for example, grassed areas or planting) meet hard surfaces. In all but the most rural of situations, an edge will be required to stop soft material leaking on to the hard. This will also create a change in level for mowing and trimming purposes in the form of mowing margins. Edges may also be useful adjacent to buildings, seats and furnishing fixings, lighting points, trees and other areas where a neat finish is difficult to achieve.

Allowing parsley and sage to spill over, hard-wearing and frost-proof bricks form a contrasting edge to a gravel path.

These yellow tulips planted between paving create a highly decorative and colourful splash for a path that is not a main route.

The smaller the unit size, the easier it will be to create complex shapes. In practice, the smallest size of material readily available is sand — which, whilst comparatively unstable on its own, when mixed with a binding agent, such as cement or resin, can be trowelled into almost any shape imaginable.

More common smaller materials are based on inexpensive gravels, available in a wide range of colours and which associate well with informal planting. These too can be mixed with binders or binding matrices, such as cement, or with resins or polyurethane to create a more solid surface which exploits the visible properties of the material.

Larger stones, such as river or coastal cobbles, granite setts or manufactured units, such as bricks, blocks and specially shaped units, can be used to create quite complex shapes. The larger and more rectangular the blocks, the more difficult they are to fit into curved and circular patterns. Units larger than 200mm(8in) in any dimension are not recommended for this sort of pattern.

Square and rectangular units, such as slabs, flagstones and large flat cobbles, are useful for making rectilinear shapes, but awkward for making curves or circles where a lot of difficult and expensive cutting will inevitably be involved.

It is possible to buy specially manufactured units, or have paving material made to order to achieve almost any shape imaginable. For pre-cast materials this comes at significant extra cost, but in natural stone may not be much more expensive than standard rectilinear units, especially if a garden designer working with computer-assisted design software is able to communicate directly with a quarry.

Where smooth surfaces are required, or where a great variety of colours, patterns and textures are needed, it is worth considering using manufactured or fabricated unit materials for the surface layer. Designing with smaller units requires the ability to visualize the paved area from the outset. This is one of the most exciting aspects of paving design, and experimenting with patterns, colours and arrangements of different sized materials can provide hours of productive enjoyment. Precedents from existing and successful paved surfaces can be copied. Pattern books, paintings, graphic design texts and artworks, mosaics and other two-dimensional pictures are also all fruitful sources of inspiration. Varying just one parameter, such as texture, but not another, such as colour, can also create subtle and more minimal effects.

Drainage channels, gulley positions and inspection or manhole covers will also affect the overall appearance and should be carefully detailed. Recessed trays are available to allow surface finishes to be taken across underground access points without interrupting the surface appearance.

A cobbled edge detail and crossfall to a gulley or soak-away carries drainage water away from a gravel path.

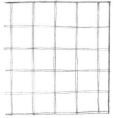

All five slabs need cutting

Extend to avoid cuts

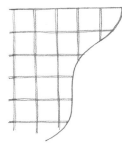

Awkward cutting with small vulnerable pieces

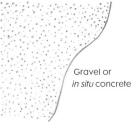

Gravel or *in situ* concrete

Thin metal or timber edges – no cuts needed

Selecting surface materials

Each material serves a different purpose. Stone paving interspersed with brick provides a smooth surface for seating, while uneven reclaimed random stones discourage a shortcut.

The strength of the wearing course comes from the aggregate or materials used. Naturally strong and durable materials such as granite will be much more robust than softer stone aggregates such as limestone. Availability of these materials will depend upon locality, stock and transport costs. Choice of aggregate will depend upon availability, properties and appearance. When granular materials are used with a binding agent, the combination of both will govern the appearance.

Using loose materials such as gravel or crushed stone

In informal situations, such as a path or drive where costs are to be kept down, loose material or gravel is useful. Although noisy when in use, this quality can also be helpful in increasing your sense of security – it may announce a person walking up a path, or the arrival of a car. On the downside, the progress of wheelchairs, pushchairs, and wheelbarrows may be slow and the ensuing ruts and grooves a nuisance to rake over.

Most parts of the world have a reasonably local and plentiful source of stone suitable for crushing into small particles, quarried gravel or other similar natural material. As local supplies are usually inexpensive and appropriate they are often a popular choice for paths, drives and other hard standing areas.

Bound gravels and hoggin These are mixtures of large stones with a proportion of fine slightly soluble material. They are laid in layers, usually 50mm(2in) thick. They are then watered and vibrated so that the fine particles

Using gravel

▸ Gravel must be angular and lock together or it will be impossible to walk on. To make the paths useable and comfortable, keep the depth of gravel to less than 75mm(3in). Use small particle sizes, 10–20mm($\frac{3}{8}$–$\frac{3}{4}$in), but not too small or cats will mistake it for a large litter tray.

▸ These materials can also be used in shady areas where grass may not thrive. Gravel forms an undemanding level background to overhanging plants, its earthy colours and inherent colour variation complementing other subtle changes in the colour of flowers and foliage, and appearing less synthetic than manmade materials.

▸ Gravel is useful around trees as it allows their roots to breathe, avoiding rigid paving lines around the trunks.

▸ It will be wise to include a geotextile layer to prevent gravel sinking into the ground. This layer will also help to prevent weed growth.

▸ Perhaps the greatest advantage of using gravel or other loose material is its ability to flow into awkward shapes and corners, rather like using a bag of sugar as opposed to lump sugar in a bowl.

▸ More angular and smaller particles which are well compacted will give strength to the surface, fitting and locking together rather like a jigsaw, in contrast to a path surfaced with a deep layer of rounded shingle, which is impossible to compact successfully.

▸ Avoid using gravel immediately around buildings or doorways where it will be frequently dislodged and will need regular maintenance. If you need to have continuity of material, consider sealing the top surface with a clear binder.

▸ Gravel is laid on a compacted base or sub-base, laid to falls and compacted with a roller to lock the aggregate together. Normal thickness is 50–75mm(2–3in) laid in a single layer.

with a 50mm(2in) base course of coated macadam (asphalt) and a 15–20mm (¾–1in) wearing course should be sufficient. The construction is the same for clear binders with 15–20mm(¾–1in) of this higher-quality wearing course being used instead of the bitumen version. The colour of the aggregate will be important. When constructing this type of surface in the US, you may be required to obtain a geotechnical analysis of the soil to tell you the exact thickness of layers to apply to your surface. Bear in mind also that this type of surface can ony be laid in favourable weather conditions, i.e. an even temperature of around 7°C(45°F).

Brick or block pavers Clay and concrete blocks are a popular choice for vehicular access, drives and more formal paths. They are attractive (especially clay types) and small enough to allow some curving of the edges without awkward cutting. They can also be used to create interesting patterns and mosaic arrangements rather like pixels on a computer screen. They are available in

Allowing plants to encroach over the edge without damaging the lawn, a brick mowing strip also doubles as a narrow path.

Older bricks weather at different rates creating an interesting patina which is difficult to replicate with new materials.

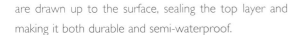

are drawn up to the surface, sealing the top layer and making it both durable and semi-waterproof.

Sealed gravels and Tarmac Gravel combined with bitumen, resin or a polyurethane binding agent will provide a useful, non-slip and comparatively waterproof surface, making it especially suitable for vehicle routes. In confined areas, power-steering will rip most surfaces to shreds, so decorative finishes and loose stones should be avoided.

Black tar and bitumen surfaces will fade to grey and become very unsightly when repaired, as an exact colour match is impossible. If access is required to underground surfaces, consider small units laid on sand. Two main systems are used: the first applying two layers of hot-rolled coated aggregate on to a prepared sub-base; the second using cold-rolled asphalt, but the result is similar. For most cohesive soils, a 150mm(6in) sub-base, covered

standard sizes or as special shaped units and come in a wide range of colours and finishes. All require edges.

Large unrelieved areas of highly manufactured and uniform pavers can look municipal. Avoid large expanses of single colours that are more appropriate to a garage forecourt.

All pavers should be frost and slip/skid resistant. Second-hand bricks have an immediate sympathy with older brick or timber properties, but may not be fully frost resistant. Some have 'nibbed' sides so they cannot be butted tightly together. This creates a small joint that is later filled with sand and helps the units to lock together. They are laid on to a prepared and levelled base, usually of sharp sand, or sand and lime to a ratio of 1:4. The sand layer is spread thicker than required so that, following compaction, the finished depth is 40–50mm (1½–2in). The units are then placed directly on to the sand in the required pattern and vibrated into the sand layer. This

A traditional fan-shaped pattern of easily laid stone sett cubes contrasts with a low brick retaining wall.

In an informal gravel path, cementing cobblestones to create obvious risers absorbs a change of level.

Large and thick, this stone paving path is heavy to lay, but is wide enough to allow plants to encroach over the edges.

forces some sand up between the units, locking them into place. It is therefore essential that the edges be constructed first.

Various patterns are common for different purposes (see page 87). Running bond is good for indicating flow and direction but gives poor resistance to manoeuvring vehicles and so is not recommended for drives. Basket weave and other grid-like patterns are most suitable for pedestrian use; herringbone pattern is recommended for manoeuvring vehicles that tend to force the units to move sideways. Rectilinear patterns tend to avoid the need for cutting at the edges, especially if the pavement edges are designed at critical spacings that correspond to multiples of full unit sizes plus joints.

Natural stone sett and cobble types Setts are cubes or cube-like units normally cut from granite. Older and reclaimed setts were quarried and cut by hand and are still quite common. They are characterized by reasonably accurate cube shapes with one smooth surface that results from many years of use. Patterns tend to be rectilinear or traditional fan-shaped in form. Stone setts will never wear out and are certainly one of the most environmentally recyclable building materials around. New setts are now split from a larger lump of stone by machine and are much less uniform in shape and rather less attractive. Most setts are 100 × 100 × 100mm(4 × 4 × 4in) but are also available as double-sized units of 100 × 100 × 200mm(4 × 4 × 8in) that are useful for edges and as nosings for steps.

Cobbles are round and should be larger than setts, commonly about 100 × 100 × 200mm(4 × 4 × 8in). When laid directly on soil or hard-core, loose cobbles are useful by trees, especially where the immediate ground level has to be raised. River and marine cobbles should be sourced carefully to ensure that indiscriminate digging from beaches and rivers has not taken place.

In construction terms both setts and cobbles are often commonly specified, laid into 50mm(2in) wet mortar on to a rigid concrete slab or 100mm(4in) lean mix sub-base. In most instances, and unless heavy vehicular traffic is required, it is best to follow the lead of our ancestors, laying them directly on to compacted soil

and brushing soil into the joints. If the soil is stony they are better laid into sand in much the same way as for pavers. Construction principles are similar to pavers but because their dimensions are less regular, the base and bedding layers may need to be varied to fit in the units. Traditionally, 10mm($\frac{1}{2}$in) joints are usually left in between the units and brush-filled with sand or soil.

Slabs and flags Natural stone and pre-cast concrete slabs are highly suited to larger areas of paving where they can be used to make rectilinear shapes quickly and easily. Natural stone is the most prestigious of all paving materials and, apart from clay bricks, the only one that will actually look better with time. Aged stone is impossible to mimic, although technology in the development of cast slabs has improved dramatically in recent years. Natural stone can become almost jewel-like when wet.

Pre-cast units are either soft moulded when they are weak, especially if new; or they are hydraulically pressed when they become exceptionally strong. Once cut, both

types never look quite right and so the design must use whole units. One exception is high quality reconstituted stone where the structure is uniform throughout. This can be as expensive as natural stone and no substitute for the real thing, although, again, some manufacturers are producing very high-quality products and useful modular versions where designs can be based upon a kit of parts. Concrete finishes can be smooth, textured, tooled or ground to reveal the aggregate, which is then called 'terrazzo'. It is best to choose colours derived from the aggregate rather than pigments, which usually tend to look synthetic.

Natural stone is sedimentary, especially sandstone, which can have attractive banding and is comparatively non-slip if kept clean. It can be riven (split to reveal the bedding planes), sawn, shot sawn (appearing rather like corduroy) or tooled. Metamorphic rocks, such as slate and marble, must be fully slip-resistant and will need to be mortared on to a solid concrete slab. Limestone and other softer sedimentary stones may not respond well to freezing conditions in winter. Avoid thin tile-like products intended for interior use.

Sawn stone, reconstituted stone and pre-cast slabs come in uniform thickness and so can be laid quite quickly on to a well prepared bed. Riven stone can vary in thickness and it will take time to set each slab level. Natural stone is expensive if bought in identical sizes. It is cheaper if bought in uniform width, or random length or even random sizes, although a totally random layout is quite difficult to achieve.

The preparation of the sub-base is critical in flexible construction, as large slabs may crack if air space develops underneath. Rigid methods of construction will, on the other hand, allow the surface stones to be quite thin, almost like a tile, and cost savings can be significant.

Larger and heavy regular-sized sawn or cast slabs over 40mm(1¾–2in) thick can be laid directly on to dry sharp sand or a sand/lime mix and butt jointed with very thin joints measuring only 1mm(1⁄20in) or so. Thinner, lightweight slabs, irregular slabs and concrete units can be laid on to a 50mm(2in) full mortar bed on a solid concrete slab or 75mm(3in) compacted lean mix sub-base. Ensure that surfaces are kept clean of mortar.

Riven and highly textured slabs should be laid to drainage falls of around 1:40, but smoother slabs can be laid as shallow as 1:80.

Tiles and mosaics These are usually limited to small areas of special emphasis. A large variety of sizes, shapes and colours are available from around the world including natural stone, ceramic tiles, glass tiles and tesserae, river-washed pebbles, glazed terracotta, quarry tiles and other more unusual and bespoke materials. Pebble mosaics characterize many Chinese and Moorish gardens and are popular in sensory gardens and those based upon Eastern philosophies.

Most are laid on to a 100mm(4in) concrete slab cement/sand/aggregate with a ratio of 1:2:4, with 10–15mm (½–¾in) cement/sand screed (1:3) and

A star-shaped slate pattern sits well between the cobblestones.

A mosaic strip introduces variety in colour, texture and form.

joints of cement/sand (1:2) or cement-based tile grout. Thin and small pieces can, however, become dislodged or flip out if frost gets in underneath.

Timber Hardwood timber blocks which act like stone setts can be set into rammed soil or on to a sand/lime bed. A well-trafficked area with coarse-textured timber, adequate falls and good ventilation and drainage should be really non-slip, and would offer a change from many of the other heavier paving materials used. Timber slats and boards are discussed in Chapter 7.

Flexible or rigid construction

There are two ways of constructing paths and paved surfaces. The first uses layers of granular material topped with a surface layer called a wearing course. This is known as *flexible construction*, and the whole path system is allowed to move in an elastic way, usually very slightly, without affecting the stability or appearance of the surface in the short or long term. Most surfaces are constructed in this way. However, in certain situations no movement is acceptable at all. For example, if the surface were covered with an intricate mosaic, or thin tiles, then any movement would cause it to crack or break and spoil the whole effect. Also, if the ground is soft or may be likely to settle over time – very common in new built situations – cracks or soft spots may develop which could lead to unsafe or unsightly depressions, or raised edges to paving units which could collect water or cause a safety hazard. In this situation a solid base of concrete is required. This is known as *rigid construction*.

Design of a flexible path or pavement

The major principle behind flexible paving is that the downward load is absorbed into the ground, protecting surface and visible layers. Many of the decorative surface finishes are not strong enough to support the weight of people or cars without breaking or sinking.

The ground on which the paving is to be constructed may well be strong enough to take the predicted load without any alteration. For instance, flat rock outcrops will normally take intensive use and sandy, dry grassed soils may well take occasional vehicular use without

damage. If this is the case, then paving design can be based entirely on visual and contextual reasons rather than practical and physical ones, and the surface material may be placed on the surface with only minimal material added underneath to ease levelling.

Engineers test the suitability of soils by checking their bearing capacity. Rock, gravel and sand will be able to absorb greater loads than loamy and silty soils. Clay soils are the weakest, by far, and will require a greater depth of construction. Strength will be affected by the water content which may also cause the surface layers to change shape – especially in clay soils and so this weaker material may need to be removed and replaced with something more solid. In most garden situations, the load imposed by people will be minimal, and the depth or thickness of the surface material may be sufficient to absorb the load by itself.

Flexible construction layers Where this is not the case, for example in weaker soils, or where heavier loads are expected such as vehicles, additional layers of granular aggregate will be needed known as a base and sub-base.

Without changing the paving material, brick edging draws attention to the change of level between paving and water and creates a striking contrast between the paved surface, water and planting.

Their function is to absorb the weight or pressure from the surface layer, protecting the surface and the underlying soil. Continuous heavy loading can cause the material in the lower layers to lock together, removing air spaces and possibly collecting water which may then freeze and expand. A heavy roller or vibrating plate, which forces the material into compaction at a greater load than the predicted use, can be used to compact the granular material at the time of construction, so that settlement does not occur later.

The total depth of the wearing course will depend upon the thickness, the material and the strength of the soil. Typically, an overall depth of 150mm(6in) may be sufficient for walkways on most loamy or sandy soils, increasing to 250–300mm(10–12in) for vehicles. Consult an engineer or landscape architect, if in doubt.

Materials used for these lower layers should be easy to handle, to spread and compact. They should be strong and angular so that they lock together when compacted. Soluble material and weak stone is not suitable.

In most garden situations a single layer of 0–50mm (0–2in) sized aggregate may be needed up to 100mm (4in) thick. If this layer is more than 100mm(4in) thick, a second layer will be needed below, which can include material up to 75mm(3in) in size and can be as much as 300mm(12in) thick in soft clay soils.

The base and sub-base provide an accurate formation for the wearing course. Because the lower layers tend to be made from larger aggregate sizes, which provide additional strength and ease in handling, there may be quite large air spaces into which the wearing course may work itself. In these situations a base layer comprising smaller aggregate sizes is required, using a range of sizes will help fill air spaces, and the base to lock together. Crushed stone that includes all sizes of material from 50mm–dust (2–0in) is commonly used, i.e. all material passing through a 50mm(2in) sieve. If air spaces and holes are still prominent, then a blinding layer of sand can be included to fill the voids and provide a flatter working surface for the wearing course.

It is critical that the base is constructed to accurate levels, falls and tolerances, as the thin wearing course often has little capacity to take up imperfections.

Edges to flexible surfaces

Edges may not be necessary for granular surfaces as long as the underlying layers project out from the top surface at 45° so that each layer is supported. This may be useful in informal and more rural situations.

Prevention of lateral spread Where feet and vehicles put pressure on the edges of flexible paths, the side units will become dislodged and the edges will collapse. Overall pressure away from the edge will also produce lateral forces within the pavement and will require a strong edge restraint to prevent spread or leakage of smaller granular material. Edges must be rigid even though the surface may be flexible.

Rigid pavings are not subject to the same lateral spread and therefore do not require edges for structural support. They may be included for aesthetic reasons or to collect water.

Collection of drainage water Where surfaces slope away from the centre, any edge which stands proud will collect water. The raised edge will guide water along its length and into a collection point, often a gulley. If they are

Using flexible construction techniques, a number of different materials can be combined. Setts quarried from a different region edge this stone path. Brick cross panels are used to break up the directional flow.

Brick on edge

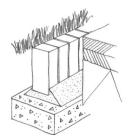

Brick on end

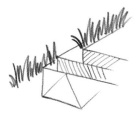

No edge

Timber board and peg

Metal strap and pin

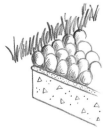

Cobbles/mosaic

designed to collect water, then they must be waterproof. In more rural situations, flush edges are useful to restrain the surface whilst allowing water to pass over them and into ditches, streams and planted areas.

Construction The construction of edges will depend largely on the situation and choice of material. However a number of broad principles apply:

The edge must be constructed first. This is crucial in flexible paving situations where the edge acts to contain the surface material during construction and after-use.

The edge must be at least as deep as the wearing and base course. A deep sub-base can extend under the edge and act as a support for it. The edge foundation will be built on top of the sub-base if levels allow and act merely to retain the base and wearing courses.

The edge must be prevented from being pushed sideways. Where the edge is constructed from large solid units, such as stone units, concrete edging or decorative units, this is usually achieved by placing lean-mix concrete against the back face of the edge, which when set will produce a solid vertical support. This is known as haunching and must be struck at an angle to shed water and allow a close fit of adjoining materials and surfaces. A 100–125mm(4–5in) haunching will be adequate in most situations. Where the edge is constructed from less solid materials, such as timber or metal, pegs or smaller vertical supports can be fixed to the back face and then hammered into the ground.

The edge must be prevented from being pushed into the ground. For this reason a foundation is often included that will sit on the sub-base or part-depth of the sub-base. The foundation should pass under the whole width of the edge material and extend beyond to support the haunching. *In situ* or poured concrete foundations need not be deeper than 150mm(6in), and 100mm(4in) is adequate in most situations. The foundation will also act as part of the edge in prevention of leakage of sub-base and base material.

If acting to collect water, the edge must be waterproof. This will normally be achieved by close butting of materials, the inclusion of concrete haunching and gathering points such as gulleys, which feed into a surface water drainage system or a soakaway.

Edging materials Simple cheap edges can be made from timber boards, butt–jointed and pegged. Timber is short-lived and cheap and is extremely useful as an edging for both of these reasons. 'In-built' decay can be exploited where, for instance, a path is to be constructed which needs to blend into the surroundings after a few years, when the path will have had time to settle and will no longer move significantly. Timber can, however, be made to last longer if pressure-treated.

Timber edge boards should be located vertically and pegged on the outside with 450–500mm(18–20in)-long softwood pegs at maximum 1m(3ft3in) intervals and where edge boards meet. Boards should be nailed or screwed to pegs at intersections.

If bends or curves are required, then thin boards 25mm(1in) can be bent by sawing a series of parallel cuts close together halfway into the board on the internal side of the curve. The boards are then pegged in the normal way. If curves are required it is better to use metal edging strips which are welded, on-site, to metal pins, and the whole structure driven into the ground in sections. Metal edging is neat and almost invisible.

For stronger and more durable edging, or where the edge forms a significant part of the overall aesthetic, then stone, brick or concrete units can be used. Stone is expensive when new and only slightly less expensive when reclaimed. Units are available in rectangular and square sections and occasionally in radiused units to achieve curves. Special shapes and sizes can be cut to order. All of these will require concrete foundations and haunching.

Pre-cast concrete units are cheap, utilitarian and can also be obtained coloured or with exposed aggregate. Many versions are available from builder's merchants, but again, curves are not widely available. Pre-cast concrete edges for footpaths are also available. These are almost all 50mm(2in) wide and 225, 205 and 150mm(9, 8, and

6in) in depth; lengths vary from 300–1200mm(1–4ft) Alternative depths can be made by cutting 50mm(2in) paving slabs or for an exposed aggregate/rough textured edge by snapping the slab. Rounded and bull-nose sections are also available. They are not available in curved sections and may have to be cut into short lengths to negotiate curves. All require concrete foundations and haunching.

Clay units are available, mostly in modular units which work with other products from the same manufacturer and are useful for matching or contrasting different products. They have differing durability designations that should be checked. Because they are small, they are useful for negotiating bends and curves. Specials can be manufactured to order or selected from a limited range in catalogues. Ranges of colours are also available. Shaped and moulded patterns can be found in both traditional and contemporary designs but will require concrete foundations and haunching.

Many other materials can be used for edging including plastic, glass, cobbles, rough stones and sculptural artefacts. As long as they are durable, securely fixed and prevent lateral spread and leakage, they should work.

Design of a rigid path or pavement

Where the soil is of very poor quality, where it has recently been moved around or where the surface is thin or fragile, rigid paving, made from concrete, often needs to be specified.

Concrete is very strong in compression but quite weak in tension. It is critical that the concrete pavement is supported under the whole of its underside. If this does not happen, then point loadings may act on the area leading to potential failing. In order to prevent this from happening, the strength of the concrete is often increased by the inclusion of steel reinforcement towards the base of the slab.

Rigid paving is useful because it can cover areas under a single construction and 'iron out' weak areas, making it useful on made-up, badly-drained, and weak ground. However, unless it is faced with another material, concrete is not attractive as a surface outdoors and will require specialist labour and heavy machinery on site.

Because surface facing materials are not taking any load and are fixed rigidly into place, a far greater variety of materials can be used to create more patterns than is possible with flexible pavings.

Construction of rigid paving For practical purposes, slabs which are reinforced should not be less than 100mm (4in) thick. This allows sufficient concrete to cover the reinforcement. Because the slabs are high in the ground profile they are susceptible to frost attack. The design of rigid paving must therefore allow ground water to drain away from underneath the slab. This is achieved by laying it on a drainage blanket of free-draining granular material or sub-base.

Slab thickness will vary according to the expected use and load-bearing capacity of the sub-grade. Typically slabs of 100–250mm(4–10in) are used with 100mm(4in) being suitable for most garden applications if it is reinforced or 150mm(6in) if it is not reinforced. Concrete of a compressive strength grade of up to about C20P (3000 PSI) is suitable. For non-vehicular areas, such as a garden path, 75mm(3in) of concrete laid on to 75mm(3in) of compacted sub-base should be sufficient. For vehicle access and driveways 150mm(6in) concrete on to 100mm(4in) sub-base should be laid if not reinforced.

Expansion and contraction joints Concrete cannot absorb thermal expansion and settlement following curing and drying without cracking. If the stresses become too great to be absorbed by the slab then it will break. To allow the slab to crack in a controlled way and to absorb movement of the slab caused by heating and expansion, expansion and contraction joints are included. (See illustration on page 14.)

Expansion, contraction and longitudinal joints leave ugly lines on the surface of the slab, especially when filled with flexible mastic. They must also run through the full depth of construction so that they appear at the surface. They should be considered as part of the overall pattern.

Joints along paths will be needed every 3–4m (approx 10–13ft) but, in practice, pouring concrete in bays means that construction joints may be needed every 2m(6ft6in) or so. In larger paved areas include joints every 4–6m (12–17ft) in all directions. If slabs are bridging weak ground liable to settle over time, consult an engineer who will recommend how to prevent the slabs settling differentially. Concrete will not set in very cold weather and may require the use of concrete blankets for it to set properly, or waiting until the temperature increases.

Concrete finishes If there is no added surface material, then it is possible to achieve a finish to the concrete slab that is both attractive and slip resistant. However, exposed aggregate concrete has the top layers of concrete washed or brushed off when still 'green' to expose the internal aggregate structure. This relies on high-quality and attractive aggregate together with a careful concrete specification so that the aggregate does not sink to the bottom. This creates a slip-resistant finish. Tooled finishes include trowelled-smooth surfaces, or sand-blasted, or surfaces hammered, needle-gunned or bush-hammered to expose the internal structure of the slab and create a slip-resistant finish. Sanding and planing can produce a smooth terrazzo finish which can be polished to a shiny surface. Finally, a wide variety of finishes can be achieved by using embossed formwork or moulds pressed into the surface of the concrete when still wet.

Added surface materials such as blocks and slabs are set into 10–25mm (¾–1in) wet mortar and mortar pointed.

GRADIENTS REQUIRED FOR DRAINAGE	
Materials	**Gradient**
Slab paving	1:70
Textured slabs	1:40
Rolled asphalt	1:40–1:48
Hot-rolled asphalt	1:48
In situ poured concrete	1:48
Concrete blocks/brick pavers	1:50
Granite setts and cobbles	1:40
Bound gravels and hoggin	1:30
Gravel	1:30

Tiles, mosaics and pebbles/stones can also be set into wet mortar, resin or cement-based adhesives. Expansion and contraction joints in the base slab should be taken through the surface layers in the same alignment and orientation. The slab is laid to critical levels and falls, as the surface material cannot achieve variations in height. Other materials can be set into mortar or adhesive and grouted to make a useable and aesthetic surface.

Drainage

All paved surfaces must slope. Even gravel paths will collect dust and debris over time, clogging or even sealing the surface. Drainage will be especially important close to buildings and entrances and any paving should adjoin the wall 150mm(6in) or more below the damp proof course or top of the foundation of the building. Where this is not possible, leave a gap of about 75mm(3in) between the edge of the paving and the wall and infill with clean pea shingle or with gravel.

Lay all paving with a slight fall across the surface and away from the house – allowing at least 50mm(2in) over 2m(6ft6in), In small areas or across narrow paths, the surplus water should drain off into nearby planting or a well-drained lawn. For larger or enclosed areas, a drain run linked to a soak away may be needed at the edge of the paving. If there is no space for this, the paving may need to be laid to fall to a central gulley or series of gulleys, also linked to a soak away or to surface water drainage. Recessed areas of paving can be profiled to collect and channel drainage water. These need to be on a water-proof concrete foundation, even if the area is a generally flexible construction. Many shapes and profiles of channels and gulleys are available from manufacturers.

Smoother and more waterproof surfaces will require a shallower fall, as water will pass across them more quickly. Generally the minimum gradients shown here in the box should be used.

Choosing your paving and path surfaces may present a challenge, but as they will probably be the most memorable and much used horizontal feature in your garden, it is worthwhile exploring the many different materials, how they can be used and the construction and cost implications before coming to a decision.

Embedding cobbles into concrete

Embedding is a very effective method of creating a 'personalized' path or paved area. The materials need not be expensive, and although time consuming, it is very easy to do.

First decide on your pattern and your material. Nearby, on a plastic sheet, lay all the tiles, pebbles, stones, shells, fragments of glass or whatever you want to embed.

Next mix the concrete, perhaps using a retardant to slow down the hardening process, and pour it into a small section of the path up to the appropriate level.

Wearing rubber gloves to prevent your fingers coming into contact with the concrete, first push in the pebbles to make up the main outline of your pattern. Ensure that each pebble is embedded up to two-thirds of its depth to avoid it becoming loose later due to frost or usage. Infill with contrasting materials as you go along.

Take a small section at a time as within one hour the concrete will harden. Once the concrete has fully hardened and the pattern set, spray off any debris or unwanted material.

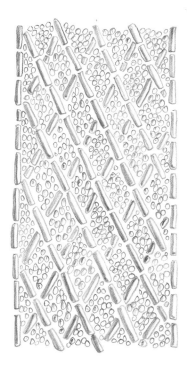
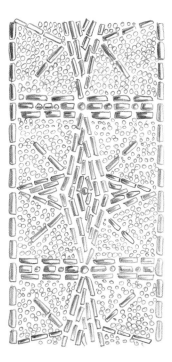

Above Such an intricate pattern of different coloured stone needs to be laid by experienced craftsmen.

Left For centuries pebbles and small stones have been used to make durable paths of simple repeating patterns. Using stones with a strong colour or tonal contrast produces the most successful results.

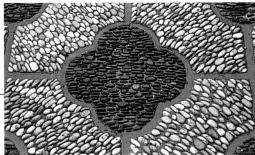

Below, left Concrete dividing strips separate the different patterns, allowing each area to be worked within a defined space.

Right Many materials, some unusual, can be used to make paths. Here beer bottle bases have been set into wet mortar.

Creating a striking design, access and changes of level are accommodated by reinforced concrete stone slabs set one above the other on concrete stilts.

A double circle of brick laid on edge defines an important transition in the gravel pathway.

Accurately cut stone and limestone chippings create a difference in texture, also marking subtle level changes.

Large section timber adds interest to a simple gravel path.

Circles of rammed earth separated by narrow strips of grass, flow round a central flint mound.

The edge of this stone path is emphasized by contemporary lighting and a stark colour contrast.

Set into a gravel path, thin stones laid on edge indicate the directional flow.

Etched into the stone panels, coloured enamel creates a ribbon pattern.

A decorative but uneven stone path slows down the walking speed.

Doubling as a mowing strip between lawn and soil, this old stone path allows plants to flop over without damaging the lawn.

Metal grid has been used as a path material to ride over uneven surfaces and planting. When viewed from above it is almost transparent.

The floorscape of large unit polished stone panels reveals the beauty of the natural material and generates interesting reflections, especially when wet.

Brick is a versatile small unit material, easy to lay and requiring minimum cutting at path junctions.

Becoming larger as the radius of the circle increases; these paving stones can be cut into various shapes.

Quarried limestone as rocks or steps bring texture and light into this Japanese-style garden.

Useful where a smooth surface is required, concrete is a rigid material which needs to be contained by shuttering, in this case, self-oxidising sheet metal.

A sawn timber log path is infilled with gravel, giving a change of texture and appearance between the timber and the cobbles.

Bold use of line, as well as strong contrasting colours and textures, together with a small detailed brick motif have been combined to great effect.

2

STEPS & RAMPS

Leading to an obvious destination, this impressive arrangement of steps and landings is emphasized and given rhythm by large decorative urns.

Previous page **Risers and treads are of prime consideration in step construction. Here a timber handrail provides support as the risers gradually turn a corner. Infills of local stone chippings create an informal tread.**

Steps & ramps are usually thought of as a way of negotiating slopes and changes in level quickly and safely. Far from simply being a functional element in your garden, steps and ramps can also fulfil an interesting decorative transition, even if they are not an absolute necessity. They can connect or define different areas of the garden or terrace and, by being steep, gentle or meandering, can control your pace through the garden. They can twist and turn, providing unexpected views or indicating a change in direction.

In most gardens, steps tend to be used for some of the following reasons:
- to prevent erosion by wear and tear of feet on soil or plants
- to force a break in the way people move around gardens, perhaps to accentuate a view or draw attention to a hazard

➤ to allow easy movement up and down slopes while keeping your foot flat. This avoids stretching weaker calf muscles at the back of the leg and uses the more efficient thigh muscles
➤ to emphasize the importance of entrances to areas or buildings
➤ to create interest and patterns

A flat site can gain a great deal of character when a change of level and steps or a ramp are introduced. Particularly in a small space, digging out a change of level can transform the existing garden and the way it is used. Two, or preferably three, steps up or down are often all that is needed.

Where to use steps or ramps

Although the main objective may be to take you safely and easily from one level to another, the steps and ramps that you create should also become an essential architectural link between house and garden.

Throughout history there have been many examples of both simple and amazingly detailed and complex steps. Contemporary designers are now experimenting with traditional materials and techniques and trying to use them in new and exciting ways. However tempting it may be to copy older precedents, often constructed from stone, remember that skilled labour is now a very much more significant part of the overall cost. One alternative is to use modern, less expensive units made to mass-produced sizes, making building quicker and cheaper, but only if they are not going to compromise the overall effect.

It should be possible to move around outdoors easily, either quickly or at a leisurely pace, which means steps ought to have shallow risers and deeper, more

A TYPICAL FLIGHT OF STEPS

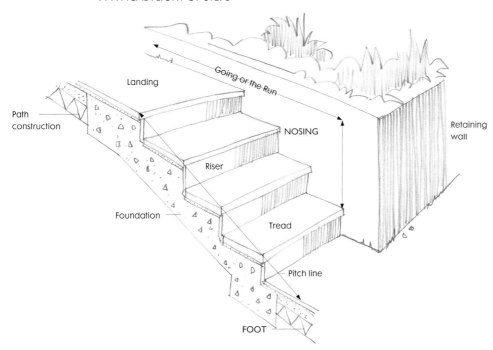

Landing

Going or the Run

Path construction

NOSING

Retaining wall

Riser

Foundation

Tread

Pitch line

FOOT

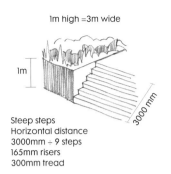

1m high = 3m wide

1m

Steep steps
Horizontal distance
3000mm ÷ 9 steps
165mm risers
300mm tread

3000 mm

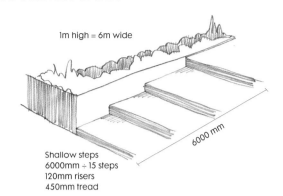

1m high = 6m wide

Shallow steps
6000mm ÷ 15 steps
120mm risers
450mm tread

6000 mm

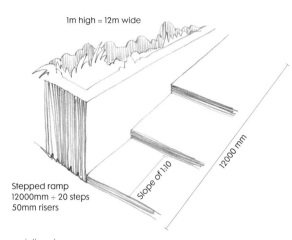

1m high = 12m wide

Stepped ramp
12000mm ÷ 20 steps
50mm risers

Slope of 1:10

12000 mm

Guidelines for steps

▸ Risers and treads should be uniformly spaced.

▸ Risers should be no less than 75mm(3in), and not more than 165mm(6 in).

▸ Treads should be no less than 250mm(10in), and not more than 450mm(18in).

▸ Shallower risers require wider treads.

▸ Set dimensions to complete a full comfortable stride when moving from step to step.

▸ Consider occasional landings — needed after 11 steps to make the going easier — which could also double as viewing points.

▸ Landings should be no less than 1m (3ft3in) wide.

▸ Where a flight projects from a raised terrace, include a landing at the top of this flight.

▸ Consider providing handrails for safety, 900mm(3ft) above the pitch line.

▸ Avoid single steps, which can go unnoticed and be a hazard.

generous treads. Sometimes a ramp is a better solution, especially where people cannot negotiate steps easily or where wheel-based travel is used. But a ramp always takes up far more space than steps and it may be very difficult to fit one into a small garden. If there is room, steps and a ramp can be built next to each other, allowing you to use whichever is most convenient.

Planning your steps

In most cases it is advisable to use steps of the same height within each overall flight. In longer flights of steps on steeper slopes is advisable to include a landing mid-way and certainly after every 11 steps. If there is enough space, a generous landing at the top of each flight will help to stop people missing their footing as they start to descend. However, these are guidelines rather than rules and for centuries designers have successfully used steps to manipulate how people move around gardens.

Deciding how many steps will be needed to cover the change in level should probably be your first consideration and will dictate the height of your risers and width of your treads. This is done by dividing the height of the bank (or vertical height difference) into an equal number of steps of a decent height (see Guidelines for steps). This number is then multiplied by the desired tread width to give the total horizontal distance on the ground that is required.

Height 800mm(2ft8in) divided by step height 75mm(3in) = 10.6 steps. Rounding down to 10 steps would give 800mm divided by 10 and a riser height of 80mm. 10 steps × 250mm(10in) tread = 2500mm horizontal distance.

Whilst mathematics will allow you to calculate the overall number of steps, their height and width, you should also consider the building materials from the outset.

Insitu concrete can be cast into any size and can be moulded exactly to meet the mathematical requirements. Timber can quite easily be cut or joined to make risers of unusual height. Stone can also be cut to size, but at considerable cost. Unit materials, bought from suppliers and merchants come in standard sizes and may present more of a problem as the flexibility of combining these materials is restricted to whole units, or minimal manipulation of the thickness of joints.

By varying the tread width and riser height steps can be made more comfortable and easier to negotiate. However, the trade-off is a significant requirement for more space.

To remove any danger of slipping on surface water or ice, there should be a slight fall on each step from back to front, or towards the edges, where water can be collected or run into surrounding ground. Careful consideration should be given to where drainage water is collected, especially at the bottom of the steps, where it can become a hazardous and unsightly puddle.

Layout and design

Although there are general guidelines for width dimensions for steps, for all practical purposes these must finally depend on the number of people using the steps, the direction of flow (or in which direction the steps are used), and the type of route. For instance, a winding woodland path could have shallow, informal, narrow timber steps, but to flank the entrance of a large country house, wide, generous, classical dimensions would be preferable. (See also Chapter 1.)

Adding a landing and slight change in direction can make a flight of steps interesting and encourage different views around the garden.

Many of the design issues that apply to the appearance of paths and areas of paving will apply equally to steps. These include opportunities with pattern, colour and texture, as well as choice of materials, locality, style and context. In addition, though, there are some important design factors which steps provide in garden detailing, worth considering at an early stage. Steps look very different when one is ascending to when one is descending. As you walk up steps you are looking at a series of horizontal lines (the risers), which may be considered quite differently to the treads. They can be in shadow or cast a shadow, can be made of the same material as the treads, or be quite different. Here is a chance to develop a vertical design statement. When decending, the risers are not seen at all and you only look at the treads. This produces another occasion for pattern, but care should be taken to avoid one step visually blending into another. There are also opportunities for subtle lighting to accentuate shadows or eliminate them.

Today most examples of garden design that we see in the contemporary landscape, especially steps, have been designed using a computer. This gives rise to designs that until very recently could not have been built, not because the technology didn't exist, but because the sheer cost of the design and manufacture would have been prohibitive. For example, a flight of steps can now be made of natural stone where every step is a different shape and size, indeed every single piece of stone is different. Forty years ago this would have involved stone masons making templates, cutting stones individually, marking them and then assembling them on site like a jigsaw. Now, one computer-assisted

Flowing curved steps invite you to use them and can be carefully located to avoid or emphasize existing features, such as trees.

Below left The horizontal lines of these gentle risers, creating a shadow, are most visible when ascending.

Below right On descent, the shadow is obscured and the pattern of the treads revealed.

Alternative design ideas

▸ Shallower risers and longer treads at the top and bottom of a longer flight can ease movement and provide a gentle sense of arrival.

▸ Tall risers and narrow treads are steep and difficult to negotiate, therefore less popular. They can be used to indicate secondary routes or where a sense of achievement is needed upon arrival at the top.

▸ By increasing the heights of risers to between 350 and 450mm(1ft2in and 1ft6in), they can double up as seats. By curving these higher steps, small arenas or amphitheatres can even be created.

POSSIBLE EDGE TREATMENTS

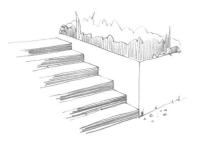

Steps built into a slope supported an edge

Steps edged by a retaining wall

Although precarious, as they disappear out of sight shallow risers and substantial treads make these steps irresistible.

design programme (design) communicates directly with another (manufacture), so that the designer is effectively communicating directly with the quarry cutting equipment. Labour costs are greatly reduced and designs can be achieved at what is still a substantial but reduced cost.

Edges and side walls

In many garden situations, steps will need to have support at their sides to contain them and to prevent material, such as soil or gravel, falling on to the treads from adjacent surfaces. Supports may not be required if the steps are free standing, for example, if they are constructed from masonry units, such as blocks, or in informal rural or temporary situations.

Side walls support the flight of steps above the surrounding ground and contain the whole structure rather like the sides of a box. These perform as retaining structures and are discussed in more detail in Chapter 4.

Edges support individual steps, cut into a bank, at their sides and prevent soil spilling on to the treads. Step edges act in the same way as pavement edges and tend to be made from materials suitable for this purpose such as brick, timber or linear sections of stone. Masonry units will require foundations and haunching, i.e. wet concrete used to support an edge unit at its side to prevent it falling or being pushed over. Timber boards will require support in the form of pegs or small posts. All can be joined or butted together if more than one step is present.

Edges on steps will collect water, as they do on pavements, and so consideration must be given to draining this water away. The edges will also need supporting and stabilizing, and so foundations will first need to be created and taken deep to meet with stable ground. Edges should not interfere with adjacent maintenance operations, such as grass cutting. This can be achieved by setting the height of the turf slightly above the edging so that the lawnmower skims over the surface.

Handrails

Longer flights of steps, or situations where missed-footing may be dangerous, will benefit from the inclusion of handrails either at the edge or in the middle. The height of the rail should be 900mm(3ft) above the steps and the rails should be smooth and comfortable. The rail supports should allow a continuous sliding of hands without having to let go. Care should be taken when specifying and maintaining timber to avoid any possibility of splinters.

Methods for attaching the handrail supports to the steps, edges or side walls will depend upon the materials and finish. (See Chapter 6.)

Design criteria for ramps

Where easy access for wheelchairs, pushchairs, lawnmowers and wheelbarrows is needed, ramps are a useful alternative to steps. However, ramps take up a lot more room than steps and, therefore, in small confined spaces, create a major headache for designers. In terms of appearance and construction they can be considered as inclined

A curved blue handrail highlights the outside edge of a shady stepped walkway, with timber risers infilled with gravel forming the treads.

LEVEL CHANGE OPTIONS

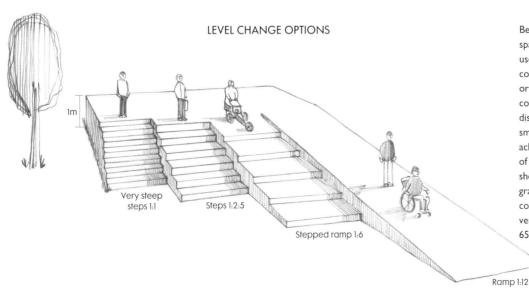

1m

Very steep steps 1:1

Steps 1:2:5

Stepped ramp 1:6

Ramp 1:12

Bear in mind mobility issues and space requirements for different users. It is possible to construct a combination of steps and ramp, or a stepped ramp. This technique connects two levels in a shorter distance than a continuous ramp, as small, vertical, level changes are achieved with risers along the length of the ramp. The wider ramp/treads should generally not exceed a 1:10 gradient, and the steps (or more correctly risers), which should be very obvious, should not exceed 65mm(2½in).

A combination of stone step and ramp caters simultaneously for both feet and wheels. A smaller scale stone inlay, which is less slippery, is used for the ramp.

paths and so the same principles that apply to paths will apply to ramps. They differ from paths at their edges where there will often need to be a retaining wall instead of a simple kerb or edge trim. It is this junction with the retaining wall that needs careful consideration.

One other significant difference is the issue of slip resistance and a non-slip surface being essential on ramps. Ensure that all ramps have a cross fall or camber feeding into a drainage channel at the sides, sufficiently steep to prevent water flowing down the length of the ramp rather than across to the sides. The surface water will need to be collected at the sides and base of the ramp in a channel. Drainage is especially important in steeper ramps made from gravel, bound gravel or crushed stone. A maximum gradient of 1:6 can be used for able-bodied people walking over short distances, although 1:10 is preferable. Ramps used by wheelchairs should have a gradient no steeper than 1:10, with 1:12 or shallower being better. In the US the minimum allowed is 1:12.

❏ Even if steps and ramps are not a practical necessity in your garden, do consider the opportunity such a change of level can provide to include an interesting and imaginative feature.

In a relaxed rural situation, detailing of steps and risers need not be so precise. An edging of angled upright stones supports this stepped ramp.

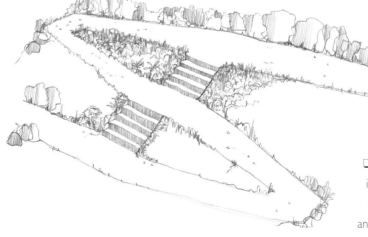

Left Ramps provide an easy means of climbing and descending slopes and should be thought of as a significant extension to the path network rather than merely a means of negotiating slopes, as they can take up 10–15 times as much space as a flight of steps.

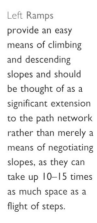

PRACTICALITIES

Constructing steps

In common with many other built elements in gardens, the construction of steps falls into two types. Flexible constructions, for example, can be used for steps that can be allowed to move slightly during their lifespan as the soil or ground settles. This type of flexible structure is cheaper, much simpler to build and especially suitable for less formal situations, such as in countryside or woodland gardens.

Where no movement can be tolerated, for example in a town garden, detailed junctions between separate landscape elements are required, then the steps will need to be constructed using rigid foundations made from concrete or blockwork.

Flexible construction

In many garden situations simple and cheap forms of flexible construction are perfectly adequate, durable and relatively easy to build. They work well in more relaxed situations, away from architectural elements and within informal planting, woodlands and meadows. At its simplest, and often most effective, flexible construction might involve cutting rough steps into soil, placing large and heavy flat or flattish stones at the front of each step and backfilling with gravel or even soil and turf. The use

FLEXIBLE CONSTRUCTION WITH HEAVY SLABS

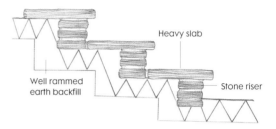

Heavy slab

Well rammed earth backfill

Stone riser

Above **Simple flexible construction using heavy slabs set on to compacted earth.**

A classic combination of stone treads and recessed risers is centred on a circular theme. Perennial daisies have naturalized into the cracks.

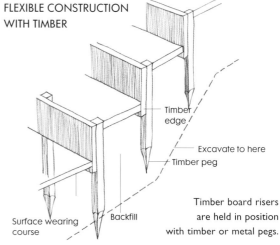

Timber edge

Excavate to here

Timber peg

Surface wearing course

Backfill

Timber board risers are held in position with timber or metal pegs.

Flexible risers The key part of this type of step is the riser. Flexible risers are constructed individually, one-above-the-other at set heights so that there is an even number of equal height risers between the top and bottom of the slope. Awkward heights are easier to accommodate as it doesn't matter as much if there is a slight difference between steps.

Nearly all flexible risers allow water and small particles through the joints, which may cause erosion of the treads through surface water run-off, as well as leaving soil particles on the tread of the step below. The inclusion of filter membranes behind the riser will prevent the passage of soil while allowing water to pass through.

Different types of flexible riser include:

➤ timber boards, at least 25mm(1in) thick, supported by timber or metal pegs driven at least 300mm(1ft) into the ground

➤ larger section timber at least 150x150mm(6x6in) or railway sleeper-sized dimensions (railway sleepers can be used but will ooze tar on hot days).

LOG-EDGED TIMBER STEPS

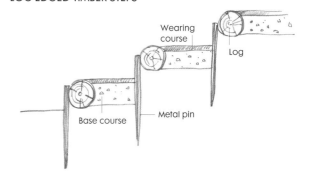

Wearing course

Log

Base course

Metal pin

Railway sleepers are used to form risers, being sufficiently robust to contain a soil tread topped with gravel. With frequent use the soil tends to erode, so the treads may need occasional renewing.

Right **A more substantial (and rural) detail using rough sawn logs and metal pins.**

of a large, heavy unit for the riser will help to keep it in place whiled also acting as a containing edge for the material used for the treads.

Flexible construction does not require foundations, although some risers may need individual foundations to prevent them sinking into the ground or settling unevenly. However, it will always be worth compacting the ground as firmly as possible before and during construction. Flexible constructions are probably unlikely to last as long as more rigid constructions and may need to be repaired at intervals.

The next few sections describe the basic principles of this type of step system. If it all looks too simple for your own situation, you may be advised to go for a more rigid construction.

▸ drystone or rubble stone material of a minimum 200mm(8in) size

▸ dry-jointed brickwork with a slab tread on top

▸ metal edging – slender and strong and can be bent into curvilinear shapes

▸ pre-cast concrete units

Flexible treads Where the treads are constructed from loose material, such as gravel or soil, they can be considered as a series of mini-pavements, held between the risers and the side edges. The principles of construction are the same as for flexible paths. In other cases, larger flat stones or slabs can be set directly on to well compacted earth so that they protrude beyond the front face of the riser. In this case use only large (at least 450mm-[1ft6in-] wide) slabs and do not include small pieces which will dislodge or wobble as the ground settles.

Edges to flexible steps The edge treatment will depend upon whether the steps have been dug into the bank or have been built over the top of the slope. In the former case and in all but the most informal situations, material will be required to fill the triangular gap between the top of the tread and the pitch line of the steps (the line that would be drawn through the nosings of each step giving the angle of the slope). Most often this will be constructed from the same material as the riser so that the steps form a complete whole. Where the steps are above the surrounding ground level the edges will act like a box, holding in the step construction material.

Rigid construction

Unlike flexible construction where some movement could be tolerated, there are many situations where the finished steps must remain absolutely stable. A high degree of control and accuracy may be needed to meet the overall exacting requirements of the design. This is especially important where different parts of the garden, such as steps, retaining walls, terrace, and most crucially of all, water, meet. A second consideration is that many desirable materials, such as bricks, stone setts, tiles, smaller stone units and mosaics, require rigid foundations. More practically, most garden construction projects requiring

steps will involve moving earth around, and this ground will settle over time, causing problems with levels and drainage, unless a solid structure is built over it, which can resist movement.

Rigid steps are much more expensive than flexible ones and may require specialist advice, methods and equipment. Large flights of steps will require large retaining structures and could even pose a problem of mass movement in the future. If in doubt, consult an expert.

The overall principle is that the foundation, risers and treads are all locked together to form a solid structure that cannot move. In some cases the side walls, or retaining edges, may also be built into the overall structure, but most often they are built separately from the steps. The construction of these edges needs to be considered early on. (See Chapter 4.)

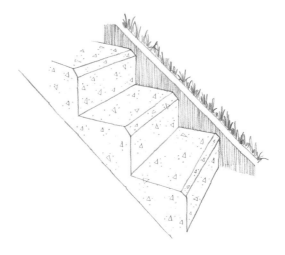

Poured (*in situ*) concrete steps can be cast to exact dimensions of tread and riser. Note that the nosing has been chamfered to prevent it breaking.

Rigid foundations are constructed from blockwork, mass or reinforced concrete.

Blockwork foundations are good in smaller gardens and in less formal situations. They are essentially a 'stepped pile' of blocks, configured to leave a top surface with dimensions of risers and treads suitable to accommodate the decorative finish. If there are going to be standard sized units (e.g. bricks, pre-cast slabs, stone setts), then the foundation dimensions will be critical. If the finish is to be a further thin layer of concrete render, then the dimensions can be generated by the arrangement of the blocks, possibly with the addition of smaller units, such as bricks and tiles, to achieve the final finished riser heights and tread widths.

In situ or poured concrete foundations are continuous structures, separated only by movement joints, if required. They should be made from concrete of 20 Newtons per millimetre (3000 PSI) or stronger. Mass concrete foundations will be thicker than reinforced and should not be thinner than 150mm(6in) in any dimension. Reinforced concrete foundations can be thinner, are better over weak ground and often cheaper for larger flights of steps. In most situations it will be worthwhile including reinforcing mesh towards the bottom of the foundation (but at least 50mm[2in] from the under surface). When using reinforced concrete to develop large or complex shapes it is essential to seek advice from a structural engineer.

Step foundations tend to be built on to slopes and are susceptible to slipping. This can be overcome by the addition of a downwardly projecting 'toe', like a wide peg, at the base of the foundation which should extend the full width of the steps and be an integral part of the foundation. A cross-sectional area of 400mm×200mm (1ft4×8in) will be sufficient in most situations, although if

When moving from light through shadow into light, stone steps approached through an arch entice one onwards, promising an element of surprise on reaching the top of the flight.

Blockwork foundations are commonly used where there are no more than four or five steps and where the flight is not very wide. With more steps, and where the flight is more than about 1m(3ft3in) wide, it will be more cost effective to use *in situ* or reinforced concrete.

The surface dimensions of *in situ* or poured concrete foundations are more critical. It is possible for the foundation and the step to be of the same structure. Here the concrete is poured into high quality formwork (the mould), of designed dimensions, so that when it is set and the formwork is removed, no further work will be required. This is known as 'fair faced' concrete and is produced through a combination of the internal appearance of the formwork, the type and colour of the concrete and the skills of the people who build it. True foundations will have another material on top and much of the work of contractors will be involved with getting the formwork absolutely right so the materials can be attached to the surface without any cutting.

In situ or poured concrete steps can be cast to any size or shape. As the flight turns the corner, the treads widen towards the bottom and drainage water will be shed to the side.

the flight is large or the foundation reinforced, advice from a structural engineer should be sought.

The addition of a large sloping slab of concrete over the surface of a slope effectively waterproofs it. Water pressure can build up beneath these foundations and can cause 'heave' (where the soil expands as water is introduced), or pass through the foundation, taking ugly cement and lime particles with it, which are deposited on the surface as permanent staining. To avoid the build up of water pressure, include an extra drainage layer of free-draining granular material, 100mm(4in) thick, under the foundation. This can connect to a land drain if necessary.

Sealing the foundation with a waterproof emulsion will prevent water passing through the foundation and surface finishes and stop the problem of staining. It will, however, reduce the effectiveness of mortar bonds especially for slender and lightweight surfacing materials such as tiles or mosaics.

Surface materials for rigid constructions In rigid steps, most of the strength comes from the foundation, so to a large extent the surface materials can be considered as decorative. Most masonry materials have to be attached to the foundation using cement-based mortar. Thinner ceramic materials may be bonded using a cement-based adhesive and grout. Other adhesives are available depending upon the materials to be bonded together.

Brick surfacing should be placed so that the headers (short sides of the brick) are perpendicular to the nosing. The nosing is the most vulnerable part of the step and most easily damaged. Small tiles and other smaller light-weight materials should not be used close to the nosing as they will break up and fall off under normal wear and tear, leaving dangerous and unsightly holes.

Surfaces for ramps As mentioned earlier, ramps can be treated in much the same way as paths, so for a discussion of suitable surfaces for ramps, see Chapter 1.

In this series of terraces, handsome flights of wide stone steps are offset by planting, their vertical 'going' emphasized by clipped yew and box. The width of the steps is reduced by the placement of seasonally planted clay pots.

Weathered timber steps demand little attention, merge with brick or other natural materials, and should be treated with preservative unless hardwood.

These shallow stone steps have an obvious overhang and huge pots to define each landing.

With minimal jointing, bricks laid on edge are a suitable height and width for these curved steps. A similar colour gravel is used below.

A rendered and painted wall edges these natural stone steps. Note the impact of the shadow caused by the overhang.

A buff coloured brick is used for both terrace and steps here. It is important to ensure that all bricks are guaranteed frost proof.

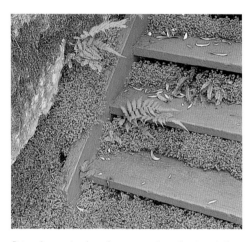

Painted or stained to show up against planting, timber softwood steps are an inexpensive solution for small changes in level.

Three stone flags, each the same dimension, bridge the width across these steps, the joints between creating a strong directional flow line.

Built as part of a wall surrounding the pool, these limestone steps form an integral part of the circular design.

Well-worn grey polished stone cobbles give texture to the treads between these shallow log risers.

Seeding into cracks between these timber steps, ferns blur both the edges and the change in width of the two short flights.

A gradual slope is emphasized by carrying a stone step across each width, with the grass area between spaced at regular intervals.

Steps can act as a pivot, changing direction as they move round corners. Shallow steps are less hazardous for this change in direction

A well-defined combination of stone riser and slate tread, with the steps becoming generously wider towards the bottom.

Shallow risers need wider treads, making the 'going' gradual and comfortable over a large area.

Blue brindle brick steps, set into a red brick retaining wall, merge with a similar wide stone coping to double as additional seating.

A poured concrete ramp faced with clay pavers also acts as a path. A drainage channel to collect water is placed across the bottom and softened by planting.

Leading to a metal deck, a curved metal ramp swings up over the planting and the pool beneath.

Roughly hewn and enduring, stone steps are cut into natural bedrock with the sides of the steps being part of the same stone.

cast dark shadows, causing uncomfortable damp areas. Where space allows, it may be better to use a series of lower walls, staggered one above the other, which will be less oppressive and allow in more light.

Another common use of retaining walls is to create raised beds which can help divide the garden into distinct areas, increase soil depth or soil type for particular plant growth requirements, and give easy access for the elderly, partially sighted or for those in wheelchairs.

Choosing which type of retaining system to use should be based on the following considerations:

- the type of material to be retained
- the height of the structure
- the shape of the structure
- the materials from which it is to be built
- ease of access
- whether mechanical diggers can be used on the site
- overall costs balanced against the amount of use it will get

The design might also be influenced by the context. Urban, strongly architectural, construction-based approaches and those that require a high degree of stability may demand very rigid, resilient structures constructed from masonry, concrete or metal. Whereas in rural situations, or where less control is required, simpler more informal solutions might be more suitable, for example the use of large heavy stones and timber-based structures.

Steel sheets, such as this self-oxidizing material can be welded, shaped or bent into long retaining walls. Because of their strength, they can achieve a structural effect with the minimum material.

Capable of holding back whole hillsides if correctly designed, massive heavy stone walls can also support steps. A thin soil trench allows agapanthus to flourish, softening the hard line between wall and steps.

Raised beds

Raised beds can also be built using similar construction methods. Such beds are especially useful in particular outdoor situations, such as courtyard, roof or basement gardens, where there may be no available soil to sustain plant growth, the entire area sometimes covered in concrete or other hard surfacing; often with essential services, such as drains or electrics buried underneath. Even where soil is available, there may be good reason for raised beds. The soil might simply be a thin layer over rock or chalk, where any nutrition – water or plant food – for plant growth would soon leach away and be inccessible to the plant.

Where soil is inadequate, you may wish to defy nature and grow plants, such as acid-loving heathers or

CHANGING LEVELS & CONTAINING EARTH

New more widely available materials and methods of manufacture have meant that designers can experiment with non-traditional means of retaining earth, such as this elegant design with its crisp contemporary detail.

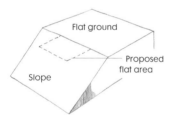

Requirement for flat land

Landform option

Retaining wall option

Changing levels & containing earth are necessary because the surface of the Earth is rarely flat. Even in urban areas, gardens often slope, sometimes very steeply. When the gradients are too steep, sloping land may be a problem for the owners, who may prefer level ground for aesthetic and recreational purposes. In this chapter we look at a variety of ways to change levels including earth-moving and the use of retaining structures. Using vertical or near vertical devices to hold back ground at steeper gradients than are naturally stable creates retaining structures for banks, steps or ramps, raised beds or terraces.

Throughout history, many of the most memorable gardens have been characterized by flat terraces and platforms, sitting one above the other on sloping sites, separated by vertical changes in level in the form of walls or earth banks. This approach to garden layout was popular in the European gardens of the Renaissance and, before that, in the classical gardens of the Roman and Greek Empires, North Africa and Asia Minor. Whilst we rarely have the opportunity or funds to construct gardens on this scale today, the impact of slicing the land into horizontal planes to exert extreme control over it and to develop a highly architectural response to the site potential, remains as important to garden design today as it has ever been.

Retaining walls and other structures are very expensive and time consuming to build and if not constructed properly have a huge potential for failure. If space allows, then, a landform option might be better and is certainly likely to be very much cheaper.

Previous page
Holding back soil at the upper level, this decorative retaining wall is the centre of the whole composition. It is separated from the lower level by a water channel. Arching steps bridge the space between while the retaining wall and carved water masks are lit subtly from below.

Retaining structures tend to be used for the following reasons:

➤ *Re-grading the landform to achieve the required levels would take up too much space.* As the graded material will have to remain naturally stable, for many materials this will mean gradients of 1:2 or shallower; so for every 1m(3ft3in) change in level, 2m(6ft6in) of horizontal land will be used. By contrast, vertical retaining structures will use a minimum amount of land to achieve the same height difference, perhaps only the thickness of the structure itself.

➤ *Retaining walls enable a highly controlled and architectural use of design.* By using a combination of retaining walls, steps, water cascades, terraces, balconies, and balustrades, designers can create a powerful three-dimensional space.

➤ *They are required as support walls to steps and ramps.* Steps and ramps are essentially terraced and inclined paved areas that need supporting edges. Where the steps and ramps need to be kept in place, retaining walls may be used.

➤ *They are required as containers for growing plants.* The construction of raised planting beds is one of the most frequent uses of retaining devices.

➤ *They are required as containers for water.* Many garden pools are edged by waterproof versions of retaining walls. (See Chapter 9.)

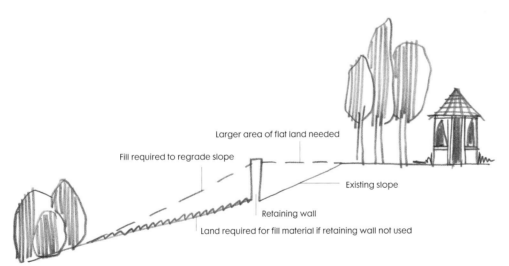

Larger area of flat land needed

Fill required to regrade slope

Existing slope

Retaining wall

Land required for fill material if retaining wall not used

Additional fill material is required to support a new raised area. This will have to be found or imported. Retaining walls mean that less land is needed and the requirement for fill is reduced.

If any retaining walls over 1.2m(3ft11in)-high are to be constructed, the services of a fully qualified structural engineer should be sought. Even for lower walls it may be advisable to use a qualified professional if ground conditions, soil mechanics or the behaviour of groundwater are not fully understood.

➤ Are you sure that a retaining structure is the most suitable solution? Does space and access allow for reshaping the ground as an alternative?

➤ Will the structure cast large shadows and create uncomfortable damp areas, especially close to buildings? If so, would a series of smaller terraces be better?

➤ Is there enough material on site to achieve the required levels? If not, where will this material come from? If too much, where can it be dumped?

➤ How high will you need to build the structures to achieve the desired levels? Are you confident that the levels can be achieved within your knowledge, or should you bring in an expert?

➤ Have you considered the most cost-effective way to achieve the change in level? For example, will the addition of steel reinforcement save materials? Would using an expert contractor or design professional give you confidence that you have made the right choice?

➤ What materials should you use? Are they reflected within adjacent buildings?

➤ If no movement in the structure can be tolerated, what type of rigid construction system should be adopted — masonry, concrete, sheet metal or rigid timber?

General principles in re-grading slopes:

➤ Natural slopes tend to be concave (dished), rather than convex (arched), as material tends to slip downhill over time.

➤ Rounded 'lumps' are rare in nature – the glacial drumlin (a long oval mound of boulder clay) is an obvious exception.

➤ Natural edges are rarely sharp, and usually 'rounded' through processes of erosion.

➤ Sharp angles will need careful soil reinforcement.

➤ Gradients must be comfortable and safe. Paths, vehicle routes, parking and games/sports areas should meet recognized gradient standards and surrounding levels at access points. Grass slopes should be planted, unless suitable for mowing and maintenance operations. Cylinder mowers can be used (with difficulty) on slopes up to 1:2 (30°) and hover mowers up to 1:1 (45°).

➤ Slopes must be stable and protected from erosion by rain and physical wear.

➤ Drainage of surface water and ground water should be designed for.

➤ At all times, healthy plant growth should be a priority; or, if topsoil is to be built on (as in a paved terrace), it should be stable, strong and compact.

➤ Topsoil on site, if good, is one of your greatest resources and certainly may be critical if you wish to be grow native plants. Topsoil should be stripped first and stored until needed.

Re-grading slopes and combining earth-moving with retaining structures

Re-grading slopes provides a subtle, sympathetic and often much cheaper means of creating useful flat areas than incorporating expensive and unnecessary retaining walls or other devices, and so should be considered first of all. Changing slope gradients can make movement within the garden easy and comfortable and can provide locations and plinths for garden structures, thereby creating the foundation for the whole garden composition.

Changing levels can involve a combination of earth-moving slopes and retaining devices and should respond to site context and overall design. A garden in a hilly landscape might allow changes to topography – perhaps reflecting natural systems – in a way that goes almost unnoticed. In a flat featureless landscape, by contrast, any landform change will be obvious. There are two main approaches. The first exploits natural slope shapes and topographical forms to create mini natural landscapes within gardens, but this is extraordinarily difficult – a discipline only really developed in the best Chinese and Japanese gardens. The second method uses precedents from landscapes and earthworks that arose through social and cultural, religious and pagan expression; through agricultural operations and control over the human landscape – especially in the architectural gardens of advanced civilizations, up to the middle part

Creating terracing by shaping the earth naturally, without walls, is often a more sympathetic and less expensive landform treatment, but the slope should not exceed the angle of repose.

of the twentieth century. Mostly such landscapes were developed as stepped terraces in, for example, Italian Renaissance gardens and classical hanging gardens, but were also created for more practical, agricultural or irrigation purposes – for growing rice, vines and tea in rice fields, vineyards and tea plantations. All are dramatic and many very beautiful.

Retained slopes also associate well with buildings and have a strong tradition in ceremonial earthworks, such as pyramids, and ziggurats as well as earth fortifications and building plinths – ditches, moats, castle ramparts and ha-has.

Furthermore, the latter part of the twentieth century, and indeed the first few years of the twenty-first, have seen landform being used in a much more sculptural way – inspired by a series of ideas and precedents that are more individual and much more difficult to define. For example, the work of land artists, such as Michael Heizer, Walter De Maria, Robert Smithson, Isamu Noguchi, Robert Morris and Richard Long, and land-based artists, such as Andy Goldsworthy, and, more recently, designers working with the landscape, such as Charles Jenks, Martha Schwartz with Peter Walker and Kathryn Gustafson, have encouraged designers and artists to work with earth as a modelling medium to express ideas.

Both the shape of the land and the retaining wall relate to the surrounding landscape. Choice of materials and the way in which they are used are crucial to the success of such bold features.

How retaining structures work

To help you decide which type of structure to use, you need a basic understanding of how retaining devices work. All retaining structures hold material at an angle that is steeper than is naturally stable, but not everything held behind a retaining wall is unstable. Imagine a vertical retaining wall holding back some soil. If the wall were taken away, only some of the soil would collapse — you would see a slope with some soil slumped at the bottom. The slope would have settled at an angle that was naturally stable (the angle of repose), so that the wall would only really need to have retained the soil now (hypothetically) slumped at the base the slope. Retaining structures, then, need to retain just the wedge of earth that occupies the space between the slope that is naturally stable (at its angle of repose), and the back of the structure itself. It is this wedge constantly pushing at the structure that can bend or break it. So the structure must be stronger, bigger or heavier at the base to withstand the pressure. There are three main forces that a retaining device needs to overcome, all of which are dependent on the degree of water pressure at the back of the wall. The first is a horizontal force whereby the wedge of earth pushes at the structure sideways. The second is an overturning force, by which the retained soil can push the wall over. The last is a bending force, whereby a wall can be bent until the material itself snaps. In most gardens these forces are overcome by fairly simple construction solutions.

Plants such as the perennial daisy enjoy seeding into cracks in this high rubble stone wall. Built with a slight batter inwards for stability, its solidly constructed corners help stabilize the structure. A slim coping stone that extends just beyond the upright surface of the wall prevents water from running down or staining the surface.

LIMITING SHADOW

High retaining walls will cast a long shadow. Stepped terraces allow light into the space and prevent shadowy areas.

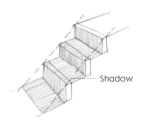

Means by which retaining walls resist natural forces

▸ *By making the structure heavy.* The overall mass of the structure is pulled downwards by gravity so that if the downward gravitational force is greater than the horizontal pushing force, the structure will remain stable.

▸ *By providing a wide foundation.* Here the friction at the bottom of the foundation helps to cancel out the horizontal sliding force.

▸ *By making the structure strong.* The forces pushing against the back of a retaining device will cause it to bend slightly. This can break mortar joints or cause materials to snap, especially those that have little tensile strength, such as concrete and masonry. Strong tensile materials, such as timber and steel, can be used instead or, in the case of steel, added as reinforcement.

So why not always make strong, heavy and wide structures? The reason is that they are very expensive and use a lot of material and labour. It might be much more cost effective to use a minimal amount of masonry, which is poor at resisting bending and therefore not very strong, but to combine it with a small amount of steel, which is very strong indeed. In this way a slender, but strong, wall can be made much more cheaply. But because it is lightweight it will still need a wide foundation.

The other key issue is the build-up of water pressure. An impervious structure is good at retaining earth, but will also contain water. The build-up of water trapped behind the wall will put increased pressure on the structure and may cause it to fail. It is critical that this is not allowed to happen and so water-proof walls should have drainage incorporated behind them, in the form of a land drain or a three-dimensional vertical drainage blanket, or water should be allowed to pass through the structure. Ensure that water passing through the structure will not collect on adjoining surfaces, causing a hazard or an unsightly stain. Dry stone walls, gabions and timber walls all drain naturally.

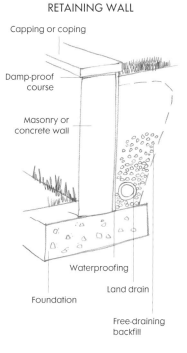

Capping or coping

Damp-proof course

Masonry or concrete wall

Waterproofing

Land drain

Foundation

Free-draining backfill

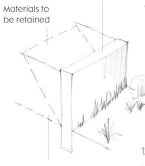

Retaining wall

Materials to be retained

Ground naturally stable below this line

Choice of retaining structure

The most common use of retaining structures is to push back and support a steep bank in order to create useful space. If this leads to a high wall above eye level (which will vary between different users), then the wall will seem overbearing and may also

As a foil for the lawn and planting, crisply detailed, light-coloured limestone is used for low walls, paths and steps, the neutral colour contrasting with the darker greens of box and yew.

cast dark shadows, causing uncomfortable damp areas. Where space allows, it may be better to use a series of lower walls, staggered one above the other, which will be less oppressive and allow in more light.

Another common use of retaining walls is to create raised beds which can help divide the garden into distinct areas, increase soil depth or soil type for particular plant growth requirements, and give easy access for the elderly, partially sighted or for those in wheelchairs.

Choosing which type of retaining system to use should be based on the following considerations:

- the type of material to be retained
- the height of the structure
- the shape of the structure
- the materials from which it is to be built
- ease of access
- whether mechanical diggers can be used on the site
- overall costs balanced against the amount of use it will get

The design might also be influenced by the context. Urban, strongly architectural, construction-based approaches and those that require a high degree of stability may demand very rigid, resilient structures constructed from masonry, concrete or metal. Whereas in rural situations, or where less control is required, simpler more informal solutions might be more suitable, for example the use of large heavy stones and timber-based structures.

Steel sheets, such as this self-oxidizing material can be welded, shaped or bent into long retaining walls. Because of their strength, they can achieve a structural effect with the minimum material.

Raised beds

Raised beds can also be built using similar construction methods. Such beds are especially useful in particular outdoor situations, such as courtyard, roof or basement gardens, where there may be no available soil to sustain plant growth, the entire area sometimes covered in concrete or other hard surfacing; often with essential services, such as drains or electrics buried underneath. Even where soil is available, there may be good reason for raised beds. The soil might simply be a thin layer over rock or chalk, where any nutrition – water or plant food – for plant growth would soon leach away and be inccessible to the plant.

Where soil is inadequate, you may wish to defy nature and grow plants, such as acid-loving heathers or

Capable of holding back whole hillsides if correctly designed, massive heavy stone walls can also support steps. A thin soil trench allows agapanthus to flourish, softening the hard line between wall and steps.

alpines, that require a particular type of soil. Or you might want to grow Mediterranean-type plants, such as cistus or lavender, which revel in thinner soils with quick drainage. Alternatively you might wish to create a raised pool, which is often less expensive than disturbing solid foundations. Where soil is unsuitable, herb or vegetable plots can also often succeed in raised beds, their structure disguising the use of grow bags for tomatoes, courgettes and gourds.

❏ There are many advantages, particularly for the elderly or disabled, in having the soil of their choice nearer to hand, and when eyesight begins to fail, the closer proximity of plants makes them easier to enjoy.

Coppiced wands of willow, hazel or other woody stems can be woven into low retaining devices suitable for raised beds. Driven into the soil, stout upright poles keep them in place.

PRACTICALITIES

Simple retaining structures with some movement

Dry stone walls

These work as retaining structures because they are heavy and allow water to pass through them easily. But it is not possible to build a totally vertical retaining wall out of dry stone, as it would fall over. However, by sloping the wall slightly back into the bank, 15° from vertical (known as 'a batter'), dry stone walls can be safely built up to about 1.5m(4ft11in) in height, provided they are skilfully constructed. In many parts of the world dry stone walling is a traditional technique and, where funds allow (the cost of labour is expensive), dry stone walling can make a strong and positive contribution to the landscape.

If the height of the wall exceeds six times its thickness, then advice should be sought from a structural engineer. Walls of 1.5m(4ft11in) in height should be at least 250mm(10in) thick. Larger stones, sometimes known as 'through stones' should be included at vertical intervals of about 500mm(1ft8in) so that they project into the bank. It must be remembered that any dry stone construction will increase its strength as the stones settle over time. Therefore concrete strip foundation, which prevents settlement, should be avoided.

Drainage is not essential as the wall will be porous. However, if there is a potential problem with soil being washed through the wall and accumulating at the front, then a geotextile filter should be placed securely behind the wall to prevent this.

Gabions

A more modern version of the dry stone wall is the gabion. Named after the French for 'cage', the gabion is essentially a rectilinear wire cage containing stone. Gabions are erected as square or rectangular boxes that are filled, by hand, with locally available large stones, usually of uniform size. Gabion mattresses are shallower and useful for retaining sloping ground adjacent to running water. All are extremely heavy and work by gravity and friction, pushing down on to the subsoil. They can be easily used in gardens up to 2m(6ft6in) in height and give a good contemporary finish. However, it remains to be seen how long these structures will last. When the wire eventually corrodes, the stones may fall out. If they are to be located close to buildings or where collapse would

cause a hazard, professional advice should be sought. Geotextiles can be placed inside the mesh so that smaller stones and/or soil can be incorporated in order to grow plants. Although artificial irrigation may be needed, gabions are free draining.

Modular systems

Many of these systems are now available and most are made from interlocking pre-cast concrete or timber units. They are suitable for structures of up to about 15m (48ft3in) in height, although if above 3m(9ft9in) or so, engineering advice will be required.

They are permeable to water and provide a number of soil pockets for planting on the front face of the structure. But because they are steep, water will drain rapidly through the structure and may become unavailable for

Right **Rectilinear cages or gabions can be filled with large local stones, gravity and friction keeping them in place. Plants will naturalize in the cavities.**

Heavy walls of dry construction will be stronger if they lean into the slope, as the centre of gravity is behind the base of the wall.

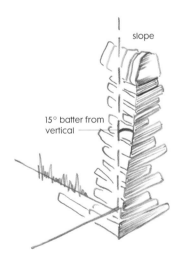

slope

15° batter from vertical

plant growth. In such circumstances, irrigation or a selection of drought-tolerant species may be required.

Modular systems, which are gravity-based, comprise of lightweight units combined with heavy backfill, and come in a range of sizes for different applications. They are battered on their front face (meaning that the front will not be absolutely vertical but will incline back) so that each layer is fully supported. Strip foundations between 150mm(6in) and 250mm(10in) thick are needed for

small structures, of up to 2m(6ft6in) in height, which should be battered to set the angle at which the structure is to be constructed. All modular systems are different and manufacturers' catalogues should be checked for specifications and recommendations. Drainage to the back of the structure is necessary in all but the most rural of situations.

Crib walls are made from interlocking, pre-fabricated timber or concrete units to create a three-dimensional grid which is filled with stone. The grid provides a frame and the stone, which is very heavy, stops the retained earth falling over. If the stone is mixed with soil, and water is available, planting should be possible on the front face of the wall.

Plastic and organic meshes and grids, vegetation and specialist geotextiles can all be used to reinforce slopes.

A mesh is used like a net, or even a bag, to hold soil in place at angles steeper than it would naturally settle. Meshes are cheap and useful for establishing plants. The meshes have small holes and are pinned to slopes with long timber or metal spikes. As the root systems of the plants become established, the strength of the bank is increased.

Timber walls

Timber is a good choice for retaining slopes and for making raised beds in small gardens. Timber is easy to use, readily available and can create structures quickly and comparatively cheaply. To be long lasting, structures must be constructed from treated softwood, naturally durable softwood or sustainably produced hardwood.

Two main ways to retain earth with timber

▸ *Horizontal timber boards supported by vertical members in front.* Here the timber boards run parallel or horizontally to the ground and are supported at the front by timber posts which are driven 40 per cent of their total length into the ground, or on soft ground embedded into a concrete foundation approximately 450 × 450 × 450mm(1ft6in × 1ft6in × 1ft6in).

Left Timber and concrete crib wall systems provide a flexible means of retaining earth. They work best when heavily planted so that, over time, they become 'green walls'.

A quick and inexpensive rustic effect is achieved by using stacked timber logs to retain earth. For permanence these will need to be secured by clever joints or a sturdy metal 'pin', driven into the ground of set into a concrete foundation.

Straight lengths of timber can be used vertically or horizontally to make raised beds or retaining walls. All must be fixed together so that they work as a single unit.

These work well up to 1m high. The space between the posts should be approximately 50–75 per cent of the height above ground level. Horizontal boards used in this way should be of a thickness of at least 75mm(¼in).

Horizontal boards should also be joined so that they act as one unit and the whole structure will be stronger if it is tied into the bank. The lowest board should be sunk into the ground to prevent any soil leaking out at the base. Drainage is important and, in order to prevent soil spewing out on to adjacent surfaces, a geotextile filter to the rear of the wall is a useful addition.

▸ *Vertical posts butt-jointed and driven into the ground.* Timber posts or logs are set vertically or at a batter, so that 40 per cent of the post is below ground and 60 per cent above the ground.

The thickness of the posts should be approximately 12–15 per cent of the height above ground level.

It is important that vertical timbers are connected to create a solid and integrated unit. Horizontal boards can be screwed to the front or back face of the timber; tongue and groove boards can be used, or the boards can be connected together with wires or metal rods. Whichever method is used, it is crucial that the timbers cannot move differentially as this will create weak points and leakage.

Rigid retaining structures for where movement cannot be tolerated

In areas where the design demands a more architectural response, or where a high degree of control is required (as in edges to steps or close to buildings), it is better to opt for a rigid structure, although it will be significantly more expensive. Rigid structures tend to be made from masonry or *in situ* concrete, although in some larger or more complex gardens reinforced blockwork and even reinforced concrete may be more cost effective.

Foundations Basic rules dictate that any retaining walls constructed from bricks and blocks need foundations that extend below the frost line, but rest above the water table. They should be built on to undisturbed and stable soil. The width of the foundation should be roughly 60 per cent of the height of the wall. So for a wall 1.2m (3ft9in) high, the foundation will be 720mm(2ft4in) wide. Depth of foundation will depend upon soil conditions with 400mm(1ft4in) adequate in many situations. Reinforced concrete walls will have integral foundations and different rules will apply.

Drainage Drainage is achieved by placing a free-draining granular material behind the structure that extends the full height of the structure. Water will then fall through this drainage layer by force of gravity, to be collected at the base in a drainpipe. These can be perforated plastic or clay, concrete or other forms of pipe that are

Below Using reclaimed vertical timbers creates a sense of durability and permanence, enhanced by the scale, proportion and varied heights of the timber.

connected to the site surface water drain or a soak-away. Special 3-D filter layers are now produced which attach to the back face of the structure and perform the same task without requiring large quantities of stone. Weep-holes, which merely spew out soil and water, are not recommended adjacent to paved surfaces.

Waterproofing The back face of the wall should be waterproofed using three coats of bitumen emulsion or by suspending a waterproofing membrane (with water-proof joints) and backfilling carefully. This prevents water reacting with salts and sulphates in the brick or mortar and also helps to guard against staining.

Thickness of rigid structures

Mass concrete, masonry and flexible structures need to have a wide base and are necessarily heavy. To counter-balance overturning forces in structures over 900mm (3ft) high, such structures must be thicker at the bottom than the top, or built into the bank with a batter of 6:1.

Brick and block walls should be a minimum of 200mm (8in) wide at the top (215mm[8½in] for brickwork and blockwork), and for the first 500m(1ft8in): thereafter increasing in thickness by 100mm(4in) for each 500mm (1ft8in) increase in height, up to 2m(6ft6in). So a wall 1.5m(4ft8in) high will be 200mm(8in) thick at the top and 600mm(2ft) at the bottom. Foundations should be twice the thickness of the base and a minimum of 200mm(8in) deep (500mm(1ft8in) where frost might be a problem). Walls up to 900mm(3ft) high can be successfully built one brick thick or 225mm(9in). No damp-proof course should be included at the base of the wall, although a damp-proof course under coping will be necessary to stop water penetrating the top of the wall. Expansion joints should be included at 5m(16ft3in) intervals and be need to be filled with a flexible waterproof mastic.

Mass in situ *concrete walls* should be a minimum of 100mm(4in) at the top. The thickness of the wall will then increase with depth at approximately 12:1–6:1 batter to a foundation with a width 60 per cent of the height of the wall. So for each 1m(3ft3in) in height at 6:1

batter, the thickness of the wall will increase by 166.66mm(6in), and by (83.33mm(3in) at a 12:1 batter. A wall 1.5m(4ft8in) high with a batter of 6:1 will be 100mm (4in) wide at the top and 350mm(1ft2in) wide at the base. It will require a foundation 900mm(3ft) wide. Concrete should be premixed to at least a strong C20P strength (3000 PSI). Some minimal reinforcement can be included for additional strength and to integrate the foundation to the vertical wall.

Mass concrete and blockwork walls will benefit from a decorative finish. This can be a cement-based render or a natural stone or brick leaf (thin half-brick), separated from the wall by a cavity that will also prevent any staining if the integrity of the waterproofing fails.

Reinforcement

For larger and more complex structures, it may be more cost effective if some reinforcement is added *in lieu* of additional mass materials. Reinforcing rods can be cast into concrete foundations in critical locations so that hollow blocks can be threaded over them during construction. Rods of 12.5mm(½in) at 600mm(2ft) centres are sufficient up to 1.2m(3ft9in) high. The wall is built in the normal way and concrete is then poured into the hollow tubes of the finished blocks so that it surrounds the rods. Hollow brickwork can also be used where the bricks act as a permanent container for the poured concrete. Expansion joints are needed at 25m(81ft) intervals. Another system involves leaving vertical 'pockets' in the rear of a nominally 225mm(9in) thick wall against which reinforcing bars are placed. The pockets are filled with cement grout and the whole of the wall waterproofed. Brick walls up to 3m(9ft9in) in height can be constructed in this way at comparatively low cost.

From the information given in this chapter, it will be obvious that, before you decide to build any retaining structures, it is worth ensuring that you fully understand the logistics. Much of this comes with experience, but if you are in any doubt at all, seeking the advice of a professional is preferable to providing an unsatisfactory solution, for which you could be held personally or professionally responsible.

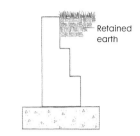

Retained earth

Masonry retaining wall

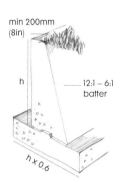

min 200mm (8in)

h

12:1 – 6:1 batter

h x 0.6

In situ concrete retaining walls

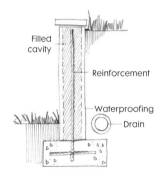

Filled cavity

Reinforcement

Waterproofing

Drain

Grouted cavity-retaining wall (cross section)

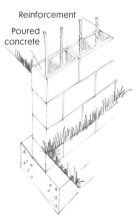

Reinforcement

Poured concrete

Grouted cavity-retaining wall

These rustic poles are deliberately angled into the bank with a unifying horizontal timber board or wire to keep them stable.

Reclaimed timber is cheap and easy to install. It works especially well with informal planting, gravel surfaces and natural stone.

Naturally oxidizing steel, such as Cor-Ten steel, weathers to a rich dark purply-brown. It can be shaped and bent and works well with a warm colours.

Poured, formed or *in situ* concrete can be cast into almost any shape. Here it is used to create flowing terraced curves which lead to a single retaining face.

Sheet material can be sliced and bent to create subtle curves and unusual planting pockets, allowing a lot of vegetation to be squeezed into a small space.

Strong plastic sheet, heat welded or bent into shape can retain small volumes of earth and is suitable for making planters and planting pockets.

Butt-jointed timber set into the ground allows water to pass through the joints and creates a neat raised edge. Note the detailing and chamfered edge.

Willow or hazel wands can be woven into retaining structures using traditional basket-making techniques. Green timber will re-grow if kept well watered.

This unusual arrangement of reinforced concrete walling, faced in brick, could be adapted on a smaller scale to a steeply sloping site.

Rough rendered blockwork and weathered timber creates an informal structure that works well with a variety of materials.

A low stone wall with flat coping is effective as a raised bed, but could equally well act as a surround for a formal pool.

Mortared stones with a sloping or battered face give this wall a solid engineered appearance, creating an overall effect of permanence and reassurance.

Mild steel straps woven between metal pins create an effective and free-draining edge to this low raised bed. Other metals, plastic or hardwood strips could be substituted.

This preaching pit at Gwennap in Cornwall has for over a century survived as a lesson in design simplicity. Dry-stone walls support turf terraces which act as both steps and seats.

Curved clay brickwork, combined with a precast concrete coping, produces an informal raised planting bed.

Stone filled mattresses which hug slopes retain earth and prevent erosion. They are a dramatic addition to a design, but are expensive.

Rusted wire and stone in this gabion combine to form a rich composition. Their weight and free-draining characteristics make them ideal for retaining earth.

Sectioned timber held in place by clever joints or metal pins can be worked into modular or rectilinear planting beds.

CHANGING LEVELS & CONTAINING EARTH **69**

4

WALLS

Why choose walls

Since walls are an expensive option, and complicated to build, they should be selected for good reasons.

➤ Strength: Walls are usually made from stone, masonry or concrete. They are solid, and offer significant protection from vehicles and noise, and effectively control movement.

➤ Durability: They are long lasting, and may re-pay their costs through enhancing property values, and through minimal maintenance/replacement.

➤ Contribution to landscape: Building a wall shows long-term vision and commitment. Walls have a relatively high apparent value — they look expensive.

➤ Energy storage: In hot weather, masonry walls will gain heat and later release it, enabling a wider range of plants to be grown.

➤ Local barrier style: Walls and walling materials may help to define an area or architectural style.

Walls are the building blocks of homes and towns. Their permanence should command respect. Many display great effort and craftsmanship. It is no surprise, therefore, that throughout history some walls, such as the Great Wall of China, the Western Wall in Jerusalem and the Berlin Wall, have become specially significant and are seen as powerful symbols of religion or culture. Walls have defined kingdoms, towns and cities. Outside towns, walls surround fields, protect livestock and give a pattern to the landscape. They also express wealth, since walls can be expensive to build and historically only the richest landowners had the money to enclose their estates and gardens.

Walls define the boundaries of many town and city gardens. They help to protect property and may be the most dominant feature in a small garden. They can provide privacy, shelter and shade, but also capture solar energy in the form of heat, releasing it slowly into the evening. In larger gardens walls can be used as separating elements to create distinct areas, divided by barriers, and visual screens – perhaps perforated by windows and doorways.

Inheriting a beautiful wall is a great responsibility. It is very doubtful whether many of the walls built up to the middle part of the twentieth century would be affordable today. Intricate brick walls, dressed stone and subtle drystone walling techniques have given way to rendered blockwork and panel fencing in an attempt to save money.

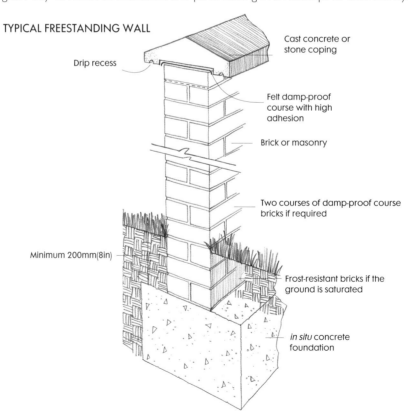

TYPICAL FREESTANDING WALL

Cast concrete or stone coping

Drip recess

Felt damp-proof course with high adhesion

Brick or masonry

Two courses of damp-proof course bricks if required

Minimum 200mm(8in)

Frost-resistant bricks if the ground is saturated

in situ concrete foundation

Traditional materials, which tend to look even better with time, have been replaced by more temporary structures that tend to deteriorate rapidly. In busy urban areas these less permanent barriers, which command little respect, are liable to abuse.

A new wall should be thought of as an investment. A good wellbuilt wall will out-live a timber fence many times over. It will make a positive instant contribution to the garden and could last for many generations. It will enhance property values, provide strength and protection and a reassuring permanence which cannot be achieved with fences. Like all good buildings, it should improve with age. Remember, though, that walls have two sides and will make a substantial contribution to the character of the area beyond the garden, too. This involves responsibility on the part of the designer, home or landowner.

Architects, landscape and garden designers have become interested in new materials and techniques that are suitable for wall construction and wall finishes, and

Gaps and openings in walls can dramatically change a composition. The curved arch gives an enticing glimpse of the pool beyond, the anticipation being heightened by the curved path. Note that the brick pavers and the shallow risers of the steps flow in the same direction.

Key design questions

- Is the wall mainly for practical or aesthetic purposes?

- Are privacy or security important? How high or strong does the wall need to be?

- Are materials suggested by locality, nearby buildings or neighbouring walls?

- What contribution will this wall make to the local area?

- Are materials suggested by the chosen design style?

- What design opportunities might arise from choice of pattern, texture, scale, relief/shadow, combined materials and unit joints?

- Will a new wall affect your neighbours? What will their side look like? Will it cast shade on to their garden?

- What are the legal, planning and code requirements?

- Is the wall protected from the detrimental effects of water, especially freezing, at the top and bottom?

- Are the foundations suitable? What are the ground conditions? In difficult soil, especially clay, would a fence or hedge be a better option?

- Will the wall be strong, or thick, enough to withstand wind loadings?

- Have thermal and shrinkage movements been allowed for once the wall is complete?

which should be considered. These include glass, gabions (metal cages filled with stone), sheet metal and timber-clad blockwork. There has also been a popular rediscovery of very ancient walling techniques such as rammed earth, cob and mud block.

The function of walls

Walls share many common functions with other barriers such as fences and railings including boundary definition; controlling movement of people, animals, vehicles and objects; visual and acoustic screening; and climatic control (sunlight, temperature and wind). The fundamental difference is that walls connect with the ground continually along their length and therefore require careful design and understanding of ground conditions. Most fence systems only meet the ground at intervals, where posts are located, and are more adaptable to varying ground and soil. Fences are also much cheaper. Walls need not be high to function as legal boundaries or to mark edges, suggesting where people should walk, for example.

Locality, craftsmanship and pattern

Walls define a landscape probably more than any other single hard landscape element. Until transport systems were developed, allowing heavy materials to be transported cheaply and quickly, walls would have been built from local materials determined by local geology. In areas where limestone is the natural bedrock, grey or white dry stone walls would be characteristic; if the local stone were slate, then black, blocky

Coping (or finishing) details are important when building any wall. The strong angular shape of this simple rubble walling is dramatized by a concrete coping painted white.

walls or walls made from thin tile-like pieces would dominate; areas of chalk would give rise to knapped flint panels; if the land were clay, then walls would be made from bricks; and where no suitable stone or masonry material could be found locally, the walls could be replaced with fences or hedges or, as in the southwest USA, adobe construction might be utilized.

Even within a region, variations can be quite marked. In the East Anglia region of England, especially in Cambridgeshire and Bedfordshire which overlie clay or gravel, brickwork walls are common. In Suffolk and parts of Essex and Norfolk, which rest on chalk, flint walls and combinations of flint and stone are more frequent while the borders between these areas will have walls made from both brick and flint. The whole area is no larger than 129km(80 miles) in any direction.

It is not only the materials that will give the wall its appearance. The way in which these are combined can have a dramatic effect. Chapter 1 on Paths and Paving deals at some length with the way in which building materials can be combined to make interesting patterns, and many of the principles described in that section

apply equally well to walls. Patterns on the vertical surfaces of walls, however, can be subtly different and more fragile as they are largely decorative and do not suffer the pressure of feet or wheels. These vertical surfaces provide one of the best places in gardens to show craftsmanship or to display artworks or artefacts.

Patterns tend to arise from one or more of the following design opportunities: firstly, by combining materials of different colour, texture and size together into a single composition; secondly, from the patterns made by the joints between the individual units; thirdly, through the application or removal of material at the surface of the wall, including the use of paint, mosaic, plaster relief or carving.

Simple rendered blockwork can be given a decorative detail by removing the top layer of render before it fully dries.

Laws, regulations, codes and being a good neighbour

There are more legal disputes about boundaries than about any other landscape or garden element. Walls are usually governed by strict planning regulations and codes, and careful checks with local authorities should be carried out before anything is built or knocked down. Regulations cover height (1.8m[5ft11in]-high is the maximum in the UK) and sometimes appearance and construction, especially in conservation or historical areas. Without permission, avoid copings that overhang neighbouring land.

Most importantly, consult your neighbours and get agreement (in writing) before you do anything. Remember that your new wall may look beautiful from your side, but may turn your neighbours' garden into a cold, shadowy box.

Where space allows, buttresses give strength to walls. Here a raised motif is repeated at regular intervals between the buttresses, creating rhythm and making the rendered and painted wall a dominant feature.

Copings, capping and creasings

Brick, concrete, stone or clay units are often used at the top of walls. They can serve practical reasons – protecting the wall from water – but can also act rather like a picture frame – helping the overall composition. Proportions and materials are important: thin pre-cast concrete units can look cheap; large units can look top-heavy.

Many masonry materials are vulnerable to damage by water, especially if the water is absorbed by the wall and allowed to freeze. Water can enter the wall as rainfall (or snow) from above, or by capillary action from the soil below. The water landing on the top of the wall has the most potential for damage, as it will be drawn downwards

Traditional coping details can be used in a variety of ways. Ridge tiles and creasing tiles are used here to shed rainwater from the sides of the wall, and to prevent it from seeping into the structure.

by gravity, deep into the brickwork where it can cause problems of freeze/thaw damage and staining. If frost is not a problem in your area, then waterproofing measures may not be necessary, but additional materials may still be added to the top of the wall for framing purposes, or to help the overall proportions. Some materials, such as frost-resistant bricks, are not susceptible to frost damage and may not need to be protected.

Copings are larger units, normally made from pre-cast concrete or stone which sit on top of the wall and shed water from its sides. They are held in place by gravity unless large or cumbersome, in which case they may need the additional security of metal dowels set into the top of the wall to prevent sideways movement. Special shapes are often adopted which are peculiar to different regions. Clay copings and colourful glazed ceramic units are popular in some parts of the world.

Cappings are mainly decorative and finish flush with the sides of the wall. They are made from one or more layers of brickwork, usually laid on edge to form a soldier course. The bricks must be fully frost resistant. Special, shaped bricks are available which are more decorative and avoid a possible problem at the end of the wall, where the last brick is vulnerable to being knocked-off. Bricks below the capping must also be frost resistant.

Creasings are a combination of bricks and clay tiles where the tile part projects over the edge of the wall to shed water away from its sides. A wide variety of effects can be created and creasings may be characteristic of a particular area.

Even though most of the water will be shed, some will pass through the joints into the wall. If using non-frost-resistant materials, a damp proof course (dpc), or vapour barrier, will be required.

Traditional stone walling types

Before the transport revolution of the eighteenth and nineteenth centuries most walls were built from local material. Stone is extremely durable and usually long lasting; because of its high cost it also gives the impression of expense and prestige. Even if it is used sparingly, the inclusion of some natural stone can transform a garden.

OPTIONS FOR THE TOPS OF WALLS

COPINGS

Stone or concrete coping

dpc

Drip recess

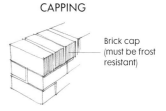

Stone or concrete coping

Drip recess

dpc

CAPPING

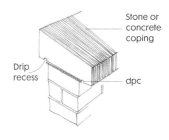

Brick cap (must be frost resistant)

CREASING

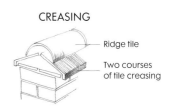

Ridge tile

Two courses of tile creasing

Using stone as a building material involves degrees of refinement ranging from a reinforced earth bank or a rubble-based agricultural drystone wall, through to the best ashlar stone; beautifully dressed joints can be almost invisible. Angular and irregular stone may require mortar to hold it together and, because the joints will be much more visible, the colour, shape and texture of the mortar will become important. Dressed or tooled stone can be very expensive, especially if the skills of a stonemason are required. For this type of project it will certainly be cost effective to use a professional skilled in specifying stone.

Reconstituted stone, made from stone dust and cement, is an alternative to consider. The material is much cheaper than natural stone and the prefabricated units fit easily and accurately together with minimal mortar joints. In terms of appearance, there is no substitute for the real thing. High-quality reclaimed material is rare, very expensive and there is always a nagging doubt about whether the material was really reclaimed or just 'claimed'.

Drystone walls

Drystone walls are perhaps the most beautiful of all stone walls and have historic origins dating back thousands of years. They are especially suited to rural areas close to quarries where they can make an important link between garden and

Retained earth bank

Drystone wall

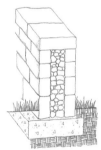

Coursed rubble wall

Dressed stone wall

Left **Locally available stone can be used to make walls and to reinforce the sides of earth banks. Over time, the stones will settle and lock together, with plants seeding themselves in the crevices.**

A low retaining wall backed by a higher freestanding wall. A coping of brick laid on edge relates one wall to another, also giving definition to the rendered finish of the higher wall.

countryside, working well with native and informal planting. But, they will always look odd in towns. Many have their origins as 'consumption walls' arising from the gathering of stones from the land. Reinforced banks and raised hedge banks filled with rammed earth and with planted tops are common in Devon, Cumbria and Cornwall. However, the two-sided freestanding drystone wall that defines fields, marks land ownership and protects livestock is the most replicated.

The construction of drystone walls (and nowadays their repair) usually involves the erection of a 'walling frame'. This is a simple wooden frame with internal dimensions that are the same as the outside of the wall. Strings are attached to these frames and lifted and re-tied as the wall is built upwards. They serve to outline the extremities of the walls and to allow the stone to be placed evenly in horizontal courses.

A well built drystone wall should have no need for mortar to cement the stones together. Indeed drystone walls gain additional strength as they settle over time and the stones lock together. Any mortar would prevent this settlement from happening. Different styles of wall are characteristic of different areas and advice should be sought from local skilled experts. Depending upon the stone and local tradition, walls may be characteristically coursed (stones built in horizontal lines, rather like brickwork), or lumpy and blocky where more rounded stones or different sized stones are used more randomly. Irish walls often have large stones laid vertically; and in other areas more complex patterns, such as herringbone, might be used. Any gates, stiles, gateposts or wall heads can be incorporated for passage points as the wall is built.

More refined stone walls

The addition of mortar allows walls to be built which are higher, more vertical and more accurately constructed than drystone would allow. If the stone is cut into rectilinear blocks the construction can be even more accurate. Rectilinear stone

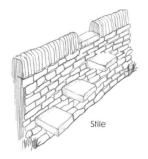

Stile

Squeeze stile

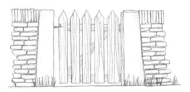

Gate set between gate posts

blocks can be laid in horizontal courses with staggered vertical joints to create a strong bond. These walls usually have stone copings or stones placed on edge at the top of the wall. Mortar joints can match the stone or become a feature of the wall, being slightly recessed or differently coloured. Dressed stone which has been carefully worked by hand or machine can be supplied or specified in special shapes and finishes depending upon the design, the type of stone and manufacturing processes. Finishes can be rough sawn, diamond sawn, ribbed, rippled or honed, chisled, polished or, indeed, any pattern capable of being cut into the stone.

Ashlar is the finest quality of walling stone and, at best, fits together so snugly that it is almost impossible to see any joints. Modern processes have made this type of stone more affordable, but it is still very expensive. In all cases, stone must be specially ordered from individual quarries, usually to a very detailed specification and cut to shapes and dimensions shown on drawings. Computer-assisted design (CAD) has reduced much of the human endeavour previously associated with production drawings for ashlar-type construction. In most stone walls the mortar joints will be significant and great care should be taken to ensure that the colour of the mortar is sympathetic to the stone. A high quality mortar can be made using stone dust available as a by-product in the quarry, and ensuring an exact match. Natural stone can be incorporated into other walls in the form of copings, quoins (cornerstones) or as decorative features.

Above **Walls can be perforated with openings or features. Here rough-sawn dressed stone is used as a backdrop to flowing water, breaking up the curved line of the boundary wall.**

Below **Facing walls with stone requires high-quality materials and workmanship. Tiles can be carefully selected to make patterns, rather like veneering furniture.**

Adding a curve can make walls very dramatic. The openings in this wall break up any overpowering effect. The slats can be of coloured glass or openings as small 'windows', any ledges being used as shelves for plants in pots.

Damp-proof courses are not normally required in stone walls, but may be added to avoid staining in more porous, lighter-coloured stone, or to avoid damage to sedimentary stone from rising salts in clay subsoils.

Brick walls

Walls have been made from bricks the world over for at least 7000 years. Highly fashionable in the eighteenth and nineteenth century, bricks fell out of favour in the twentieth century, but are now enjoying a renaissance thanks to clever marketing by brick companies, their adoption by innovative architects and a fresh interest in more traditional building techniques. Bricks are small modular units which can be put together in an almost infinite variety of patterns and structural shapes; they are easy to handle and many people are skilled in using them. Given the huge potential, it is worrying that so many brickwork walls in garden situations are unimaginative and utilitarian, showing amateurish 'standard' design and a missed potential for creating something more interesting.

Many good books have been written about designing with brick and there are countless current and historical precedents to inspire anyone who wants to use brick. Brick walls should always be considered in areas where brick is used as a building material, but they may look totally out of place in areas built predominantly from stone, concrete or timber.

The appearance of brickwork walls

The appearance of a brick wall derives from the bricks themselves (colour, size, texture), the joints (colour, size, shape, shadow), the bonding pattern (how the bricks are combined, see page 87) and the viewing distance. Selection of the bricks may be down to matching something that exists locally, for example, a house or a neighbouring wall, or bricks of different colour or texture may be chosen to allow patterns to be made. There are literally thousands of different bricks available and, because of the significant investment involved in building a wall, care should be taken to find the most suitable ones. The brick available at a local store may not be the most appropriate. You may be able to find a match at a large builder's merchants' brick library or at a design centre's library.

The joints will also be an obvious part of the wall. There are far too many examples of walls that have been let down and made ugly by horribly coloured mortar or sloppy workmanship. Pigment additives are available to match brickwork or to create a special effect. The profile and depth of mortar joints will have a very significant impact upon the overall appearance of the wall and should also be specified carefully.

The way in which bricks are bonded together will also affect the overall appearance. Traditional bonding patterns include 'stretcher bond', 'header bond', 'English bond', 'Flemish bond' and subtle variations of these. Other special construction bonds may be chosen which use less material or provide greater strength. Careful orientation of bricks into three-dimensional surface patterns can create impressive effects. The possibilities are limited only by imagination, cost and skill.

Curved walls, such as this 'crinkle crankle' wall, use minimal material, are strong and stand up well to wind, but need to be built by specialists. They occupy more ground area than straight walls, and can intrude into neighbouring properties.

Brick walls that are 'half-a-brick-thick' can only be made in stretcher bond. Walls 'one-brick-thick' or thicker can be made from a variety of bonding patterns created by combinations of 'headers' (the narrow end) and 'stretchers' (the length of the side). The choice of bonding pattern will be based upon strength, appearance and locality. It is worth experimenting with different patterns and colours of bricks, but beware of the wall becoming over elaborate.

Half-a-brick thickness is only suitable for walls up to 900mm(2ft11in) in height. Straight walls, one-brick-thick, can be built up to 1.5m(4ft11in) high.

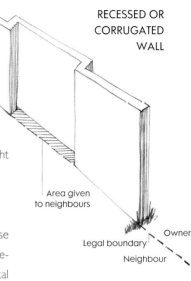

RECESSED OR CORRUGATED WALL

Area given to neighbours

Legal boundary

Owner

Neighbour

The shape of brick walls

Brick walls, and indeed other masonry walls, tend to be built in straight lines. Because of their small size, bricks also lend themselves to gentle curves. Giving a wall a three-dimensional profile has an advantage of making the wall stronger against horizontal forces, especially wind, and some very beautiful walls, known as 'crinkle crankle' walls, have been built in this way. To build curved brickwork correctly is a specialist operation and more often walls are built with piers and panels or crenellated. These last two types are less suitable as boundary walls as they occupy more ground area than straight walls and may eat into a neighbour's land.

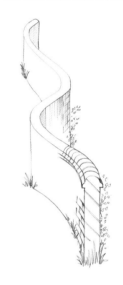

CRINKLE CRANKLE WALL

Concrete, rendered blockwork and decoratively faced walls

Traditional garden walls made from stone and brick are very expensive. Cheaper, faster and less skilful walling systems have become more popular – so much so that they are often characterized as 'modern' or 'contemporary' – and aspirational, even though their origins may be wholly down to economics. They are the only way to effectively build large flat surfaces suitable for painting and, as such, can be used to great advantage to link interior and outdoor decorative finishes.

Rendered and stone- or brick-clad blockwork

Blockwork walls are comparatively cheap to build and have a major advantage over brick walls in that they can be built quickly. Construction rules are the same as for bricks, the difference lying in their appearance. Blocks come in standard sizes and co-ordinate with standard brick dimensions so that, when combined, greater flexibility is possible in building to set wall dimensions, without the necessity of cutting hard concrete blocks. Most people choose to cover blockwork with a smooth or profiled, cement-based render, but other suitable materials include ceramic tiles, mosaics, stone tiles or timber. Some designers and homeowners are happy with a painted finish applied directly on to the blocks.

Freestanding walls made of concrete

Mass-gravity, *in situ* or poured concrete walls allow for a wide variety of three-dimensional finishes arising from the choice of framework, formwork and type of concrete used. These walls involve creating a mould (formwork) on site into

Inexpensive rendered and poured concrete walls can be finished in many different ways. A contemporary effect is achieved by abstract painting, strategically placed so that it can be viewed through the gap in the planting.

which wet concrete is poured. Constructing *in situ* concrete walls is a specialist operation, especially if they are large and reinforced; they are not recommended in most domestic garden situations where simpler blockwork walls are an easier and safer alternative. However, many new gardens include walls made in this way and it is possible to employ specialists to help realize imaginative design that would not be possible using other building techniques.

Even if the design effect or required appearance does not demand *in situ* concrete, in large areas it could still be more economic to use poured concrete in preference to blockwork. In this case walls should be a minimum of 100mm(4in) thick and the thickness should increase by 100mm(4in) for every 500mm(1ft8in) in height. The concrete mix should be C15P or preferably C20P (see Materials).

In situ concrete can be fair faced, where it is poured into a high-quality smooth or profiled mould, or finished later by tooling, texturing, etching, polishing or exposing the aggregate.

If the concrete wall is to be faced with stone or brickwork, metal ties should be cast into the wall so that they correspond with every third or fourth course of facing material, and at 1m intervals along the wall. The cavity is normally left empty. Foundations are the same as for brickwork walls.

Adding steel reinforcement to distribute loading stresses can save material, but specialist advice should be sought.

Facing concrete walls

Thicker materials and blocky materials, such as bricks or stone blocks, can be built as a thin wall adjacent to the concrete with metal ties connecting the two 'skins' to prevent them separating. Coping stones will be required and must be wide enough to cover the full width of the wall, including the cavity and any overhangs.

Thinner materials, including thin stone, ceramic tiles and mosaics, can be glued directly on to the face of the wall with a cement-based waterproof tile adhesive. Larger thin stone facings are usually hung on to special metal brackets and hooks systems, commonly used in the facing of modern buildings and which vary between different manufacturers. Timber cladding is another option that can also be added to achieve an effective, but comparatively cheap finish.

Alternative materials

It is worth considering other materials suitable for constructing high-quality and long-lasting garden barriers.

Metal sheet material can be erected quickly and, if designed cleverly, can produce a high-quality barrier which works well with planting and which can reflect heat and light into the garden. Sheet steel and Cor-Ten steel (protected by its own oxide in the form of rust) can be used and etched, cut or bent to create interesting design possibilities for modern gardens.

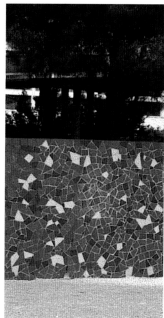

Glass blocks also produce a striking overall effect, distort views and make good separating elements without reducing light levels too significantly. They do, however, need regular cleaning to maintain their appearance. They work, and can be constructed, in a similar way to masonry blocks and conform to the same principles except that they require specialist mortar.

As designers and homeowners are becoming more concerned with environmental issues, less destructive building techniques are becoming more popular. Rammed-earth walls made from a mixture of soil, hair and straw are extremely attractive and, provided that they can be kept dry at the top and bottom, should be very long-lasting. This is, however, a specialist operation requiring the materials to be mixed and the wall constructed on site.

❏ Although costly, walls offer a huge design potential often overlooked by many designers and builders. Once you have understood the constructional elements, it is not difficult to conceive interesting and unusual shapes, patterns and finishes – your walls should endure long after the main hard landscaping and planting need replacing, and may perhaps become the most permanently memorable feature in your garden.

Painted scenes or 'Trompe l'oeil' can liven up a bare wall. Use special paint that will stand up to external use, or protect the work with a final coat of varnish.

PRACTICALITIES

BRICK BONDING PATTERNS

Stretcher bond

Flemish bond

English garden wall bond
(also known as American bond)

Foundations for brick walls

The foundations are continuous strips, normally made of concrete, which run under and support the full length of the wall. Their purpose is to transfer and spread loads into the ground and to counter fluctuating water levels throughout the life of the wall. Like all foundations, the strength and size will depend upon the ground conditions, in particular the soil type, and water conditions. All soils contain water, and the weight of the wall will gradually push this water away causing the volume of soil under the foundation to change. The volume of the soil will increase if the water freezes and so foundations should extend below the frost line.

Trees close to walls will also present problems in cohesive soils, such as clay. If new walls are to be constructed close to trees, advice should be sought from local building officers or structural engineers.

For external, freestanding walls on problem soils, it is advisable to consult an engineer. However, for most purposes the following rules should be sufficient.

▸ Only occasionally will foundations be required deeper than 750mm(2ft5in).

▸ In free-draining soils of high bearing capacity, foundations can be shallower, but not less than 20 per cent of the overall height above the foundation. For example a wall of 1.8m(5ft11in) will need a foundation of 360mm(1ft 2in) deep.

▸ The foundation also helps to prevent the wall from rotating at its base, which can be caused by horizontal loads. It therefore needs to be wide enough to help spread the load outwards. Foundations should be roughly twice the width of the wall.

▸ Where loads are low, mass *in situ* concrete strip foundations should be sufficient. Concrete should be of C15P or C20P strength designation (see Materials). With high loads, or where deep foundations will be needed, it may be cheaper to use reinforced concrete.

▸ The foundation should finish two brick courses below finished ground level, to ensure that no foundation can be seen if surface layers of soil are washed away.

▸ Foundations in cohesive soils, such as clay, which can alter dramatically in size as the water content changes, may need to be as much as 1200mm(3ft11in) deep. Would a timber barrier be more suitable?

Thickness of masonry walls

Generally masonry walls up to 2m(6ft6in) high need only be 215mm(8in) thick (1925mm[6ft3in] for brick). In practice, as the exact thickness will be based upon available building materials, rather than exact mathematical formulae, it will normally be adequate to look around at good, well built, stable walls in the area and copy them. In windy or exposed areas the strength of a wall may need to be increased. This can be done by making the wall thicker, involving more material for the same height, or more economically, by introducing corrugations or zigzags to increase its contact with the ground. General rules for height relative to thickness are shown in the table on page 88, so that a wall 1m(3ft3in) high need only be 100mm(4in) thick in a sheltered area, but might need to be 250mm(10in) thick, or a quarter of its height, in a very exposed area. Generally a one-brick-thick wall in an exposed location should be no higher than 1025mm(3ft4in). Height can be increased to 1825mm (6ft) if a one-and-a-half-brick-thick walls are used. The table broadly outlines the height to thickness ratio of a wall relative to the degrees of exposure (wind). In very exposed situations, where walls need to be very thick indeed, it may be more economical to use a different shape of wall and the advice of a structural engineer.

Another method of making walls stronger is to incorporate piers or bays which will provide a greater apparent thickness to the wall, but with a minimum of additional material.

For example, a wall 2.25m(7ft4in) high can be built one brick thick – 215mm(8½in) and be stable in a relatively sheltered area. A half-brick-thick wall (102.5mm 4in) with staggered bays at 1.8m(5ft9in) centres will be just as strong, but will only need 40 per cent of the material

Flush joint

Struck joint

Bracket joint

Recessed joint

required for the 215mm(8½in) wall. A half-brick thick wall with piers at 1.8m(5ft11in) centres will use 65 per cent of the material. For large walls, over 2m(6ft6in) high, in exposed areas, it will certainly be cost effective to employ an expert to calculate the most efficient form of brick wall. A half-brick-thick wall, with 225mm (9in)x330mm(1ft1in) piers at 3m(9ft9in) centres, can be built up to 1.925mm(6ft4in) high.

Adding reinforcement bars to hollow blockwork or to special brickwork bonds, such as Quetta bond, will greatly increase strength, with a minimal addition of extra material.

Damp-proof course (dpc)

A damp-proof course may be required at the bottom and at the top of a wall and is used to prevent water rising from the ground up the wall by capillary action (rising damp). This can cause saturation and hence frost damage; staining; and encourage algal growth although it will present no structural problem if the bricks or other materials are frost resistant. If materials are not frost resistant then a damp-proof course (dpc) at the base of the wall should be included, made from a low permeability material or frost resistant bricks. Do not use a thin membrane dpc at the base of the wall as this will be likely to interfere with the adhesion of the mortar and create a line of weakness.

A bitumen-impregnated dpc at the top of the wall is different. It prevents water, which has passed through joints in the creasing or copings, from entering the top of the wall. Very little is being supported above it, but it will still provide a line of weakness.

Mortar joints

Stone blocks, concrete blocks, brickwork, capping, creasing and copings are held in place by mortar. Mortar both glues opposing surfaces together and acts as a separating filler material, accommodating rough surfaces so that they fit together.

Mortar has a few critical functions:
- It allows all units to be jointed into a single 'solid' structure.
- It can be made to allow some minimal movement.
- It allows patterns to be created.
- It can be designed to match, complement or contrast with the main walling material.
- It is made weaker than the units to accommodate movement within the joints rather than the bricks.
- It can be mixed to different strengths depending upon application.

If the bricks being used contain more than 0.5 per cent sulphates, then SRPC (sulphate resisting Portland cement) should be used.

Movement joints

Brickwork walls over 10m(32ft9in) in length will require movement joints:

This extraordinary wall is made from stone slabs bolted to a concrete wall, but separated by rubber washers. It has become a musical instrument, used by locals to give concerts.

▸ **Construction joints** allow new bricks to take up water and expand. This is a process which can continue for up to 20 years. They should be located every 9–10m (29ft6in–32ft9in) along the wall and be 1mm($\frac{1}{100}$in) wide per 1m(3ft3in) run of wall plus 30 per cent, i.e. every 10m(32ft9in), include a joint 13mm ($\frac{1}{2}$in) wide.

▸ **Thermal expansion joints** are required in all walls whether using new or reclaimed bricks. Introduce a10mm($\frac{2}{5}$in)-wide joint, every 10m(32ft9in) along the wall.

▸ **Drying and shrinkage** of concrete blocks will require 10mm($\frac{2}{5}$in) joints located every 5m(16ft5in) along the wall.

The joints should be considered as a complete break running from the foundation vertically upwards and passing through all layers of the wall from bottom to top. These gaps can be filled with a neoprene mastic, baffle or other proprietary branded flexible joint filler. It is important not to locate movement joints close to door or window apertures.

Rendered walls

Render is most usually a mixture of cement, lime and sand in the proportions 1:1:6 and is applied in two or three thin layers. Stainless steel or plastic angles can be used to achieve accurate right-angle edges, and additional mesh or metal lathing attached to the blockwork will help bonding. Combinations of blockwork and the render coat can be manipulated, shaped and profiled to create curved walls, rather like icing a cake, but it will always be

STRUCTURE OF A RENDERED WALL

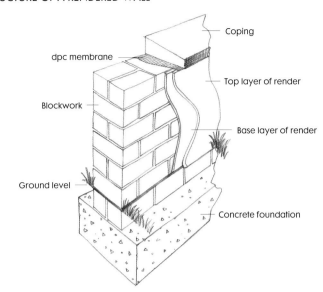

important to address the potential problem of water penetrating the top of the wall where it could cause the render to dislodge – especially if it is allowed to freeze. Copings can be added, or the render profiled or curved to shed water.

Render can also be removed or carved to develop an interesting and original three-dimensional surface pattern.

If the blocks are to be faced with brick or stone, then metal ties, which link the facing to the main body of the wall, should be set into the wall so that they correspond with every third or fourth course of facing material and at 1m(3ft3in) intervals along the wall. It is preferable to leave a cavity between the facing and the blockwork.

Copings should be considered, either to protect the top of the wall or for visual effect.

FACINGS FOR WALLS

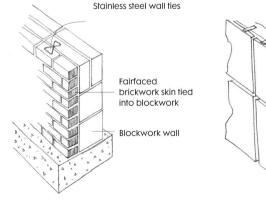

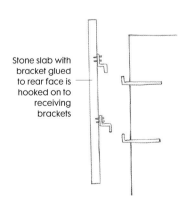

A slim metal mesh has been filled with stone and plastic inserts to create an attractive garden screen, firmly secured to the ground to prevent wind rock.

The wall face is volanic stones pushed into wet render and the patterned shape is made of mosaic.

A decorative and domestic form of 'gabion' is achieved by using metal mesh. The smaller panels are of Perspex, filled with large stones or cobbles.

Walls become animated by the play of light and shadow provided by vegetation.

An inner courtyard can be glimpsed through sliding patterned glass panels, when viewed at an angle.

Bricks can be obtained in many sizes, shapes and colours. Here the capping is separated from the wall by a decorative glazed tile creasing.

Built of 'reclaimed' materials, this wall combines varying sizes of brick and stone. Self-sown plants will help the units knit together as they settle over time.

Detailing in old stonewalls needs to be carried out by experienced craftsmen. This 'window' to the country-side beyond has captured a distant view.

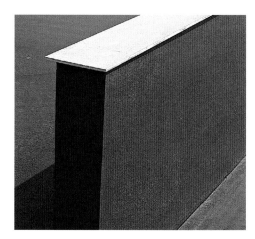

A slate finish adds a slick surface to the rendered and painted wall; the coping overhang sheds water from the rendered and painted vertical surface.

Different cultures have evolved their own style of wall finishes, developed from local materials. Earth can be moulded into various shapes and fired in a kiln, then used as a decorative capping.

The walls of garden buildings have an individual charm when decorated with terrazzo or mosaic. Buttresses project and give definition to this Italianate feature.

A highly glazed ceramic finish has been applied to this Chinese coping, suited only to warmer and frost-free climates.

Rammed earth walls have become a fashionable addition to many contemporary gardens. Created on site, these walls have a natural patina and variation.

In this circular design, transparent protection can be achieved by using curved, glass screens without casting shade or creating visual enclosure.

A garden 'room', in which the walls have been formed from lightweight plastic panels, is a technique adapted from Japanese tradition.

Slatted panels act as inserts to these mirrored walls, bringing light into the space.

High stone or brick walls can be oppressive. Creating an opening in the wall allows light and also a view. Stone columns are needed to support the frame.

Curves need to be generous when viewed in an outdoor space to compete with the landscape. Stone coping follows through the bold curved line of this wall.

5

FENCES, RAILINGS & GATES

Fences, railings or gates make the first memorable impression of any property, affecting everyone who enters. Sharing many functions with freestanding brick, stone and earth walls, they define boundaries, control movement, modify the environment and give the garden structure, shape and proportion. In some significant ways they differ from walls, and it is these differences that tend to suggest their use, in preference, as the most appropriate form of barrier. Like walls, they are crucial in defining landscape and garden and are appreciated not only by the owners, but also by everyone in the area. As they set the scene for what lies within, much care should be given to their choice.

So which is a better choice, wall or fence? Walls tend to have permenance and stability, are better at retaining heat from solar radiation, but the materials and labour costs are more expensive. Fences are cheaper, quicker to erect, can be temporary, are better at providing shelter from the wind, can be almost transparent, while still providing security and support for climbing plants. Often the budget will force the decision, although other factors should be taken into account.

A well designed fence should not exist in isolation – it should work in context with all other built elements, such as benches, tables and chairs, lighting, containers, arbours, paving, and walls. Decide whether your fencing should be dominant, as in Japanese gardens, or recessive, such as a foil for plant growth. For instance, a strong vertical pattern in slatted wood, vertical bars or even concrete is an effective contrast to the rounded outline shape of plants.

The design of your fences and railings should also be influenced by the local landscape. Rural and agricultural areas may have quite crude fences, made from simple split wood, barbed wire, or woven from twigs or coppiced canes in a random arrangement. In towns timber might be treated more formally, becoming rectangular or square in

A composite illustration of fence, railing and component types.

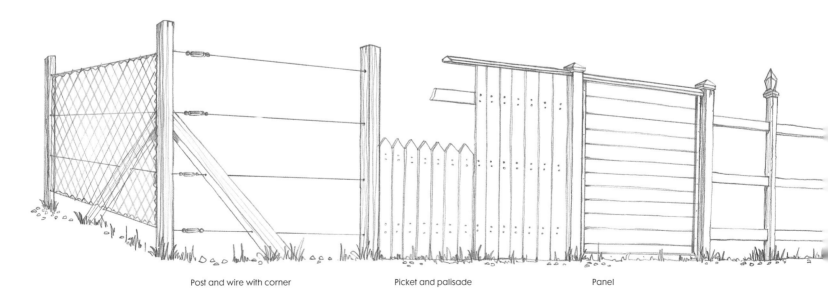

Post and wire with corner   Picket and palisade   Panel

section, and put together into fences with straight frames and panels with an obvious pattern or rhythm. In nineteenth- and twentieth-century towns, where design becomes more self-conscious, metal fences and railings might be used, with careful attention to the detailing of joints, fixings and the shape of individual components becoming important.

Because fences are made from a variety of fairly small pieces, their individual and combined shape and size will necessitate working with subtle proportions, scale and rhythm. If the component parts are oversized, timber fences can appear clumsy. Beautifully elegant barriers, using the minimum of material, are possible in metal where the same size in timber might be prone to breakage, abuse and decay. Timber comes in straight sections and is useful for making straight lines. Metal can be bent, cast, twisted, welded and brazed to form intricate and complex shapes. Both timber and metal can be painted and surface textures manipulated. Metal is chosen for inherent characteristics of colour, texture, surface appearance and finish.

Fences and railings provide occasion to include interesting opening details, such as grilles, doors and windows, giving glimpses to another part of the garden or to a distant view. Doors imply secrecy and intrigue. Low sections of fence, below eye level, maintain protection plus greater visibility. Narrow gaps at the base of the fence allow animals unobtrusive access. Louvred timber panels or slats can provide clear visibility in one direction whilst totally screening another. Slatted fences are best for diffusing the wind, while solid fences create an eddy on the leeward side, the wind passing over and down to ground level again at high speed. Slatted fences can also provide some protection against the sun, giving an attractive dappled shadow.

All fences and railings, especially those that mark legal or neighbour boundaries, must conform to your local laws and codes. Always discuss your intentions with neighbours and get their agreement in writing. Check the regulations for height and rights to light and remember that, whilst your new fence might provide you with the desired privacy and shelter, your neighbour might be plunged into darkness.

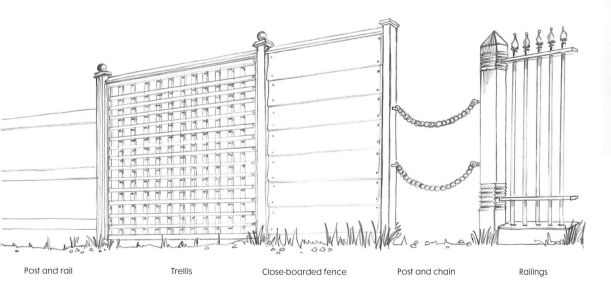

Post and rail   Trellis   Close-boarded fence   Post and chain   Railings

Functions of fences and railings

Defining boundaries for legal purposes, land ownership, land use and management.

Controlling movement of pets and people (especially children), moving objects (especially balls); preventing shortcuts.

Providing security, as fences discourage trespassers and keep property and belongings safe.

Providing screening for privacy, for controlling, framing or emphasizing views, with a choice of opaque or transparent material.

Modifying the surroundings by screening wind, noise, sunlight.

Supporting plants, training fruit on a trellis, or supporting a hedge on a wire structure.

In the USA local regulations usually require the erection of a fence if you are installing a pool.

Shapes, sizes and components

Throughout the world the general appearance of timber fences and metal railings is quite similar as a result of shared historical origins. Fences originating from defence stockades, forts and military protection, for instance, commonly evolved into palisade and picket fences, while metal railings, mostly with pointed spikes at the top, were designed to deter intruders. Agricultural fences, traditionally used for controlling stock, survive in the form of the ubiquitous post and rail fence, either as a finished fence or as a frame for vertical or diagonal boards. In areas with poor-quality building timber, woven systems were developed to include panels and hurdles. For fast, simple construction, manufactured panels, available in a kit-type form, and hung between posts set at critical centres, evolved in the modern era.

The arrival of metal wire in the nineteenth century afforded very cheap post and strained wire fences for controlling stock at a fraction of the cost of post and rail; other materials, such as mesh and chain link, could be attached. Throughout history skilled local metalworkers and craftsmen have produced some beautiful ornamental fences and gates, many decorated, in various architectural styles, with religious and pagan symbols, with patterns, shapes and motifs that illustrate stories and personalities. More recently, high-quality metal fabric, canvas, glass, Plexiglas or Perspex, sailcloth and other materials have also been used for fences. The type and form of fence you decide upon is really limited only by your requirements and budget.

A variety of high quality materials can be used to form an imaginative barrier (in conjunction with fences and railings). Translucent stained glass or plastic panels provide a point of interest in this metal grille and brings new material into the garden.

The choice of components, their arrangement and the means by which they are joined and fixed together governs the overall appearance of all types of fence. Each of these varies in importance, depending upon the type of fence system used, but it will always be necessary to consider the overall proportions.

Simple fences

The very simplest barriers, used to define edges (such as planting beds and lawns) or to control movement (where people might otherwise damage surfaces or plants), are often merely a suggestion. Bamboo, willow or other available plant stems, bent into loops and pushed into the ground, cost nothing and are often sufficient to deter, but hardly qualify as real fences. A more sturdy and permanent version, often called a trip-rail, is made from short timber posts with a single horizontal timber, metal, tube or pipe rail. The rail must be strong enough not to bend if trodden upon or knocked by a lawnmower. Paths for the blind can include a version of trip-rail, also used as a tap-rail, but which should have a smooth continuous surface, rather than being interrupted by posts.

Simplicity of design should not be confused with crude, sloppy workmanship or use of poor-quality materials, which will always disappoint and invite mis-use. Even the short-post, simple, single rail systems can have carefully considered joints and connections, dramatically improving their appearance.

Cleft chestnut fencing, made from split logs wired together, is popular in agricultural areas and parts of northern Europe and, indeed, simple post and wire fences are widely used everywhere.

Post and rail systems

Unlike post and wire fences, post and rail types have no tensile forces and are therefore simpler to conceive and construct. They are a more sophisticated, more expensive and more permanent form of barrier and are usually made from square section, rather than round section, timber to allow for more accurate joints and fixings. Cheap post and rail fences made from round peeled posts with half-round 'D' section rails can be built, but are only suitable in the most rural of situations, for example to enclose horses.

A good understanding of post and rail systems is useful as they also form the framework for palisade, 'hit and miss fences' and some panel fences.

Post and rail fences are found all over the world. They can be designed to varying degrees of sophistication but should relate to the locality and design comfort.

Post and rail fences

Posts have no tensile forces acting upon them and because the whole fence is much heavier than post and wire, they require simpler ground fixings. Posts will normally be located between 2 and 3m(6–10ft) apart, but since they are still subject to horizontal forces, should be concreted in at intervals of around 10m(approx 33ft) in the same way as post and wire fences, particularly if ground conditions are poor or the situation is exposed. Ends of runs and changes of direction should have strong ground fixings. If rectangular posts are used, place the longer axis in line with the direction of load (or wind). This also means that the longest axis will be perpendicular to the rails allowing mortises to be cut into the widest part.

Use 100mm(4in) section posts in preference to 75mm(3in). They look more substantial and have nearly twice the cross-sectional area, making them much stronger.

Rails are the horizontal members of a fence, which connect the posts and create the physical and visual barrier. They are easy to climb and are sometimes even used as seating, so need to be strong enough for this. For a simple post and rail fence, use 100mm(4in) posts and 38x100mm(1x4in) rails. Rails with a depth of 75–100mm(3–4in) and a width of 38–50mm(1½–2in) are generally suitable.

The location of the rail, relative to the post, will significantly effect the overall appearance, especially if additional timber components are to be attached to the rails to make a more complicated fence. If the rail needs to be flush with the post, for example to receive some cladding across the whole of the front face, then the rails should be housed into a notch of exactly the same dimensions as the rail. Cutting a mortise (or slot) into the side of the post and threading the rail through is a more elegant solution. If the fence is to have pales (vertical timbers) attached to the front face, locating the mortise exactly the same distance behind the face of the post as the thickness of the pale boards, will allow the whole fence to finish flush with the front of the fence. If the pales are the same width as the posts, the posts will not stand out physically or visually.

The top surfaces of posts and rails should be cut at an angle or capped to prevent water settling and developing as rot.

A typical post and three rail timber fence.

Inspired by the curved outline shapes of plants in this garden, a simple slatted paling or picket fence is stained and sawn to provide an undulating edge.

The appearance of this painted solid fence is suited to formal surroundings. Note the timber cap-rail and the hinged gate, which is invisible when closed.

Palisade and picket fences

This is the traditional type of fence identified with both the English and American cottage-style garden, which would look out of place in an urban context. Essentially the same as the post and rail type, except that they have additional vertical timbers, known as pales, attached to the front (and sometimes back) faces. They vary greatly in height and are more difficult to climb than fences with horizontal crossbars. As the pales are put close to the ground, pets are kept in and unwanted animals kept out.

The size of the vertical gaps between boards will largely be determined by the degree of permeability needed for visibility or to control wind. The optimum percentage permeability to reduce wind and create a comfort zone on the leeward side is about 20–30 per cent, so that this extent of the finished fence should be in the form of air gaps; however, 30 per cent is not a high proportion of the surface area and will not create a very private space. Where wind is not a problem, but privacy is, the gap size can be reduced to around 10 per cent, so that 100mm(4in) boards might only have a 10mm(¼in) gap. Experiment with proportions until it looks right and try to make all gaps the same width.

An alternative is a 'hit and miss' fence that allows the effect of wind to be reduced, but maintains an opaque private screen. Rails are located centrally within the post and boards are attached front and back at alternate spacings. The whole fence can be capped with a wide, shaped section of timber to frame the top.

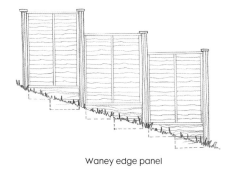

Waney edge panel

Close-boarded panel

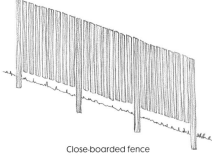

Close-boarded fence

Panel fences must step down slopes and will produce triangular gaps below, which need to be filled with timber or stone. Post and rail types with added vertical boards can follow gradients more sympathetically.

Vertically or diagonally close-boarded fences

Where there are no gaps between pales, the boards can clad the rails and be thinner, rather than provide pales at regular intervals. This is the most common type of fence (other than panelled fences), typically used for privacy.

The boards may have a uniform thickness or can be tapered, when they are known as shiplap. Other thinner boards, such as weatherboard and tongue and groove, can be used.

For neatness of appearance, these fences will normally include a caprail at the top and a gravel board at the bottom. Where a cap is used, locate the uppermost rail at the very top of the post, so that the cap can be screwed directly into it.

Post dimensions may have to be increased due to increased wind pressure.

Panel fences

Panel fences are fast and inexpensive to erect, but the cheaper, readily available versions are short lived.

There are usually no rails, as the posts are erected at critical spacings with the panels offered up to the posts and attached to the sides or front (or back) of them. Posts are moveable and easily replaceable. Before finally fixing one into postion, check whether it needs concrete footings. Because the space between the posts needs to be exactly the same dimension as the panel, posts can be harder to construct than they look. It is wiser to take your time and try not to do too much at once. Alternatively, develop your own mounting system, which includes some tolerance. Fitting a plastic spacer washer, which can be cut to length, around the screw or bolt between the panel and the post, will look elegant and save a potential problem.

Panels are not recommended on slopes. Unlike other types of fence – where posts and pales/boards are vertical, but the rails can run parallel to the ground – panels have no such flexibility and on sloping ground they can be very difficult to install. On steep ground each panel will need to step down the slope, one above the other and, even on shallow slopes, the addition of a step will be required after runs of two or three panels. Awkward triangular gaps will need to be back filled between the panel and the slope and it is easy to finish with a spoilt job.

Cheaper alternatives include woven larch panels, and wane (with some bark) edge panels which are available in 900, 1200 and 1800mm(3ft, 4ft and 6ft) dimensions. Flimsy inexpensive stapled trellis with wide apertures is available in a wide range of sizes, but is really only a temporary solution. Better quality panels include woven hazel

Rustic woven hurdles, or more refined and longer-lasting versions, such as this sawn cedar, are available as panels or can be woven on site.

hurdles and high quality trellis units which sit in substantial frames, have small aperture sizes, are made to last and are available from specialist manufacturers.

Very high quality louvered panels, and woven hardwood panels are also available. Most craftsmen will be happy to manufacture bespoke panels, which can be complex in design, but easily fitted on site. Panels made from canvas, glass, perspex, wire mesh and other materials can be made to order and often come in metal frames fixed to timber posts for easy assembly.

Trellis

In the history of gardening, simple trelliswork (referred to as lattice in the USA) must have been used quite early as a substitute for walls and hedges. Partly because it does not take up much space horizontally and partly because the panels are quick and easy to erect, trellis is now popular in all sizes of garden.

Trellis varies between simple diamond- or square-patterned, ready-made panels, often of poor quality and made of thin timber; and expensive custom-made structures in a large range of shapes, patterns, and sizes. The panels can be arranged in numerous formats, and may include intricate curved features, such as rounded arches arranged to give illusions of perspective. Look to the frontage of your house before deciding on an appropriate pattern, remembering that any ornate infill draws the eye and is more difficult to site successfully.

Panels usually come in a range of sizes up to 1.8m(6ft)-square (in the USA, they can come in a wider range), and are set on a rigid frame to give them stability. The finished panels can be decorated with timber finials, such as cubes or balls, and treated, stained or painted. Treated or stained trellis needs less maintenance, as any plants growing through an untreated trellis would otherwise need temporary removal while the trellis was repaired or repainted.

Quite intricate trellis panels, produced by glueing together several layers of wooden lathe stretched around simple fillets, can often be made by your local carpenter, and at a reasonable cost. The usual defect of trellis is a look of impermanence and improvisation, so it is worthwhile using a good craftsman.

A dark painted background provides a foil for this multicoloured diagonal trellis. Visually demanding in itself, it does not require climbing plants to complete the scene.

Many trellis and screen patterns are possible in both timber and metal.

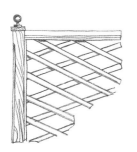  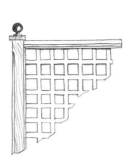 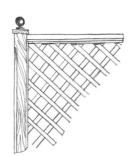 

Metal fences and railings

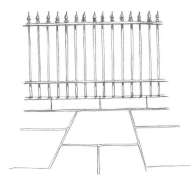

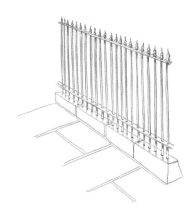

Metal railings achieve their barrier effect with the minimum of material. They are almost transparent when viewed straight on, but become more opaque when viewed at an angle.

Metal fences can be almost transparent when viewed at right angles to the line of the fence, but might be nearly opaque when viewed at an acute angle. Metal fences and railings command similar respect and prestige as walls do, but are not often used in gardens, perhaps because of their high cost. Masonry walls are solid and opaque, while timber fences are short-lived, generally limited to straight lines and panels, liable to decay and abuse. Metal, on the other hand, is one of the most flexible of construction materials, can be bent, stretched, extruded, moulded, cast, twisted, polished and welded, and connected in all manner of ways. Because it is strong, metal achieves its function, often with the minimal use of material, so that it can produce an almost transparent barrier, perhaps framing the view. Patterns are usually most effective when simple, graceful and more open than closed.

Most metal fencing available off the peg is manufactured for municipal urban use – as high security fences or as surrounds for sports facilities – most of which are not covered here. Some may be suitable for gardens, if carefully adapted. Indeed the contrast of a fairly ordinary fence with beautiful planting can be very successful.

Nearly all metal fencing is made from ferrous metals, including cast iron, steels (alloys of iron and carbon) and stainless steels (with carbon and chrome). The addition of carbon also improves resistance to rusting and causes the metals to melt at a lower temperature and so be better suited to casting into shapes. Low carbon content steels are called mild steels and can be forged when hot. Mild steels are most commonly

Metal is one of the most flexible of construction materials. Despite its intricacy, it is strong, semi-transparent, and allows light and air to circulate.

An ornate timber
and metal gate
where the braces
form part of the
design. Wire netting
at the base deters
rabbits and other
small intruders.

used to make simple garden gates and planting frames
and are used by local blacksmiths to create bespoke
commissions. Stainless steel is extremely expensive but
has enormous durability (see Materials).

Gates

Traditionally gates were specially commissioned and
had a story to tell. They were carefully crafted and,
even in a small village, no two gates were identical. In
our modern society most spatial divisions that cross a
path, track, road or circulation route will still need a
gap or opening to prevent people, especially children,
animals and pets from escaping or entering. Grasp the
chance to design your own gate to make the entrance
special, rather than choosing from a catalogue. Avoid
installing a gate merely because you need a gap. In
addition to practical requirements, gates and even
stiles (allowing people to climb over barriers whilst
deterring animals) can form an important focal point
or feature in your garden. If carefully designed, gates
encourage entry – especially if located invitingly within
a wall. The entry point should continue the rhythm of
the fence. Gates should be simple to operate and,
where appropriate, self-closing.

When choosing the size and width of a gate, bear in
mind the worst-case scenario. If emergency access is only through the proposed gate,
ensure that it is wide enough for an emergency vehicle. Don't forget that removal and
rubbish collection trucks are large. For functional purposes gates should correspond
to the widths recommended on page 105.

The construction of gates

Any gate construction will involve answering the following
questions:

- ➤ What size of posts are necessary?
- ➤ How are they fixed into the ground?
- ➤ How is the design of the gate frame to be constructed?
- ➤ How will the hinging and locking mechanism work?
- ➤ How will the gate look when viewed from both sides?

Timber gateposts differ from fencing posts. For gates over
1200mm(4ft) wide, gateposts should have a minimum dimension of
150mm(6in) in any direction, with the base of the post at least 1100mm(3ft6in)
below ground level. Typically they will be placed in concrete foundations with the

TYPICAL COMPONENTS
OF A TIMBER GATE

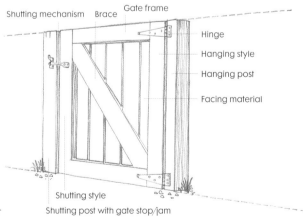

Shutting mechanism   Brace   Gate frame

Hinge

Hanging style

Hanging post

Facing material

Shutting style

Shutting post with gate stop/jam

Reminiscent of the picket fence style, the downward curve of this small entrance gate invites and beckons passersby. The finial detail is a traditional motif.

dimensions of 450 × 450 × 750mm (1ft6in × 1ft6in × 2ft6in). Metal gateposts can be narrower, but may need to be specially made to match the gate, as hinge positions cannot be determined on site.

Posts from which the gate hangs are called 'hanging posts'. Posts against which the gate shuts are called 'shutting posts'. Shutting posts can include a piece of wood or metal against which the gate shuts, called a 'jam'. Timber gateposts are usually made from oak or durable softwood such as Douglas fir or Scots pine.

Gate frame construction will depend upon the visual appearance when matching the gate to the fence or wall and the size of the gate and its required structural stability.

Timber gates

Because of the weight of the gate, square or rectangular frames will quickly go out of shape and will need bracing. In gates up to 1.5–2m(5–6ft6in) and over 1m(3ft3in) in height, a single diagonal brace is sufficient because the angle of the brace is still quite steep. If the gate becomes longer and lower a single brace will no longer be sufficient because it will begin to become horizontal. In this situation cross bracing or 'V' bracing is used. An alternative is to attach sheet-like material over the frame which may be achieved by adding paling to the front or rear face of the gate. If gates need to look the same from both sides, then the timber parts can be mortised into the frame.

It is best to purchase large, agricultural-style (or five-bar) gates from a specialist manufacturer and, if space is available, opt for a larger gate to avoid any pinch points.

The 'hanging stile', which is the part to which the hinges are attached, needs to be especially strong. The 'shutting stile' takes the lock or catch mechanism and, if necessary, can be smaller.

Metal gates

As metal gates can be made from much thinner materials they may not require diagonal bracing because the welded joints are so much stronger. It is best to order the whole set of hanging post, gate and shutting post together with all the ironmongery. Take careful measurements and build in a slight tolerance to ensure that the gate will fit when it arrives. It will be easier to polish or decorate the gate in the workshop, so be sure to specify this at the same time, if required.

Ready-made gates come with all fixings and fitting instructions, but will need finishing, usually priming and painting.

❏ Our approach to fences, railings and gates is usually fairly mundane. As you will deduce from this chapter, with imagination there are many ways of producing an innovative and exciting design, provided you grasp the potential of your materials.

Widths of gates	
600mm(2ft)	Single person
800mm(2ft9in)	Pram, buggy or bicycle
900mm(3ft)	Two people (just)
950mm(3ft)	Wheelchair
1.15m(3ft9in)	Pram plus child by side
1.2m(4ft)	Two people (comfortably)
2.1m(7ft)	Small/medium car
2.4m(7ft10in)	Large car, ambulance, delivery van, small tractor
3.0m(9ft10in)	International tractor
3.6m(11ft10in)	Fire engine, removal truck, 18-wheeler
5.5m((18ft)	Any combination of two passing vehicles

Traditional styles of gates still serve useful functions. Placed to the side of a wide remote-controlled five-bar gate, this kissing gate takes up little space and is useful for pedestrians, perhaps along a public right of way.

Fencing or trellis can be used to give additional height to an existing wall. The overall vertical dimension needs to comply with planning regulations and possible objections from neighbours.Horizontal members prevent the fence from looking too tall.

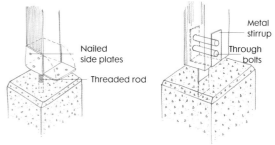

Nailed
side plates

Threaded rod

Metal
stirrup

Through
bolts

Post and footing details

Direct burial: where the post is set in earth and rammed in using backfilled material. Place some free-draining material at the base of the hole to prevent rot.

Posts set in concrete: where the post should extend down to the bottom of the concrete. Posts should be located so that one-third of the overall post length is below ground level and at least 750mm(2ft6in) deep. Dimensions of concrete footings should be 450x 450mm(1ft6in) and the full depth of the buried post.

Post anchored in a metal sleeve: which is driven into the ground or cast into a concrete foundation. This provides a quick and simple means of fixing, but is then difficult to repair or alter once fixed.

Hanging gates

Gates should always open into the property. Consider the arc formed by the gate when it is opening and closing. Is the ground flat or will the gate catch on rising land or an immoveable mound? It is important to have level ground around the gate area.

Hinges in external situations need to be strong enough to hold the gate, and set to allow the gate, if left open, to close under its own weight. The easiest way of producing a self-closing mechanism is by offsetting the top and bottom hinges so that the gate hangs at a slight angle. If the hinge is located on the front face of the hanging post, the gate will open through 180°. If located on the inside of the post, the hanging style will catch and the gate will only open through 90°.

Allow a 75mm(3in)-gap below the gate and a 10mm (½in) gap between the shutting stile and the shutting post.

A variety of hinges are available. Use strap types for heavy gates or otherwise use hinges designed for out-doors such as brass or stainless steel. 'T' hinges should be galvanized or black japanned.

The purpose of a latch or bolt is to stop the gate swinging open when closed. The simplest type is a 'Suffolk latch', which can be opened from both sides. More complex types may be 'automatic' latches that self-lock as the gate swings against them; 'spring' latches used for large field gates; or 'loop' latches that loop over the shutting stile. Ensure everyone who needs to use the gate can reach the mechanism and that it cannot be reached by unwanted intruders, or young children.

Metal finishes and protection

Because designers today are experimenting with new techniques, the results, after several years' use, can often seem disappointing. Galvanizing may break down, metal fixing to oak may rust as a result of the tannin; copper flashing may cause staining. If in any doubt, seek expert advice. Some metals, such as stainless steel, and weathering steels, such as Cor-Ten steel, which is naturally oxidizing, need no finishing.

Aluminium: may need no treatment, but is vulnerable to lime staining caused by bird droppings. It is often anodized, a process which hardens the surface of the aluminium by coating it with its own oxide.

Ferrous metals: require finishing or protecting to prevent them from rusting. Any coatings are best applied after the metal has been formed and welded.

Galvanizing: involves coating the surface of the metal with molten or a dry powder of zinc. It will then weather more slowly, but galvanizing does eventually break down.

Bright zinc plating (BZP): gives a stronger and shinier finish, similar in appearance to stainless steel.

Metal coatings: such as lead, cadmium, tin and zinc, can all be used, although zinc is the most common outdoors.

Paints and primers: including paints that need no priming. Before applying the primer or paint, first remove any oil or grease by wiping with a weak acid, then rinse in clean water. Prime with one coat of epoxy zinc phosphate primer, then two coats of finish: first a high build epoxy resin, then a final coat of enamel paint. All paint finishes require maintenance and will fade in ultra violet light.

Plastic, nylon and PVC coating: the metal is treated with an electrically-charged polyester dust, available in a limited range of colours, and fixed by electrical attraction. Plastic, nylon or PVC coating is best suited to chain-link fences.

Powder coatings: available in almost any colour, powder coatings are strong and relatively vandal proof; excellent for detailed work.

Vitreous enamel: molten glass protects the metal and the finishes are less prone to fading, the classic case being the red enamel follies at the Parc de la Villette, Paris.

Connecting metals

There are four main methods of connecting metals:

Mechanical: such as bolts, nails, screws and rivets.

Soldering or brazing: soldering involves joining by using a metal or alloy, usually tin or lead, which melts at a lower temperature than the metal to be joined. Brazing is done by using a brass solder of zinc at a high temperature.

Welding: usually achieved by pressure (as applied by a blacksmith) or by fusion (with an oxy-acetylene torch).

Adhesives: epoxy adhesives are most commonly used.

NB: Avoid bimetallic contacts, which can be corrosive. If in doubt, seek specialist advice.

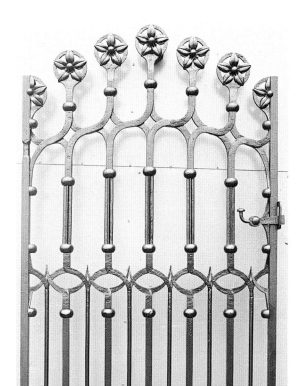

A good local blacksmith or metalworker can be employed to make original gates. Many are highly skilled and can work to traditional or contemporary designs.

109

Repeating the timber used for the Japanese garden buildings, the short timber posts here, connected with taut rope, separate the public pathway from the carefully raked gravel surrounding the planting.

Transparent heavy-duty glass panels separate the different areas of this water feature without interrupting the view.

The delicate curved pattern of the gate, inspired by its moon shape, affords a glimpse through to the view beyond. The metal hinges fixed at the edge of the brickwork control the radius of the opened gates.

A contemporary, semi-transparent circular screen of pierced sheet metal, supported by stainless steel uprights, allows wind to filter through.

Where intruders are not a problem, bamboo canes, secured together by string or twine, can indicate a demarcation line and make a subtle addition.

Timber vertical posts and caprails support this interwoven rusted metal trellis panel, the rusting iron merging with the colour of the timber.

In this metal arch, infilled with a simple metal gate, the short uprights prevent the entry of most animals.

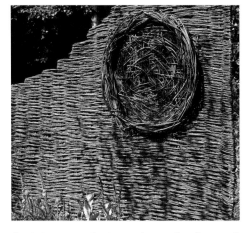

Rustic interwoven fencing panels can offer all sorts of creative possibilities in a garden, as here, where the eye is drawn to the circular woven willow motif.

Willow weaving has become a popular craft. When put in the ground, soft plant material, such as willow or hazel, may burst into leaf, creating a 'living' fence.

Rustic poles with bark left on will be short-lived but can be useful for making temporary trellis or fencing, and can even encourage experimentation.

When different types of metal come into contact, their appearance can be spoilt by corrosion. If in any doubt, seek specialist advice.

Gaps between the horizontal slats of this timber screen are filled with mirror and create the illusion of 'windows'. The slats support climbing plants.

Unless the wooden posts have been treated with preservative, this informal arrangement, separating one area from another, will only last for a few years, but it remains an effective and beautiful fence.

Inspired by hedge 'layering', coniferous sawn timber branches are set at a slant, woven through and secured onto regular upright posts. In this condition, conifers retain their bark for longer than hard wood.

Fashionable in Victorian times, cement can be moulded to imitate rustic posts, seats and other garden ornaments. Although the technique has fallen out of favour, examples still exist today.

Because of their singular nature, gates lend themselves to one-off commissions by artists and designers, such as this Jaberwocky gate by Gaudi in Spain.

Although the hanging posts are askew, the simplicity of this gate has a rustic appeal.

Separated by projecting wooden pegs, sturdy, horizontal, treated timber posts create an unusual and solid barrier between garden and garage.

6

TIMBER DECKS & SURFACES

Views from the deck should be uninterrupted if possible. A handrail, safety barrier or balustrade will provide opportunities to work with traditional, or contemporary, nautical or other themes, which can give the decking a particular character. Glass screens or infill panels can be used to create shelter from prevailing winds, but remember that any windbreak will create turbulence on the leeward side.

Types of decking

There are five main types of decking:

> Timber paths that sit directly on the ground and follow slopes and gradients; they can be constructed directly over existing surfaces providing that the new raised level will fit with existing surfaces.

> Low-level decking that provides an alternative to terracing. Usually supported by concrete piers or short timber posts, this is useful as a transition between house and garden. It can also allow a change of level, a step or steps bridging the gap between the two surfaces and, as with all decks, provides a warm surface for relaxing or for children to play.

> Decks and platforms or boardwalks that are built adjacent to, or even over, lake and pond edges. Decks that cross small ponds or streams can be considered as simple footbridges. They are especially good in environmentally sensitive areas.

> Slope or hillside decking, creating a level surface where none has previously existed without the need for complex earthworks.

> Roof terrace surfacing. This is a specialist operation so not covered here, but before beginning any major work it is wise to seek advice from an architect or an experienced structural engineer.

Construction materials

Fundamentally, timber is a renewable resource. Wood is easily worked and shaped using hand and machine cutting tools. Intricate details and ornamental flourishes can be added quickly and quite cheaply by skilled craftsmen and make a great difference to the overall finished quality of the deck. The choice of timber species is wide and each has its own performance and appearance characteristics. Timber is an insulating material and will be comfortable to walk and sit upon in weather conditions where other materials such as stone and metal would be freezing cold or unbearably hot. This is especially important in hot climates where outdoor living is a regular benefit, but where materials heat up during the day it can become unuseable. Avoid using decks in shady or damp areas where they can become slippery and hazardous.

Generally, decisions governing the choice of timber will be influenced by locality, strength, appearance, durability, ease of use (i.e. cutting, jointing and fixing), cost and availability. The appearance of the timber will be important for the parts that can be seen everyday such as the deck boards, handrail, balustrade and facia boards. The main structural components may not be seen and so decisions on what to use for these will be influenced more by strength and durability.

A wide variety of materials is available for decking – hardwood, treated softwood and naturally durable softwoods such as western red cedar. Hardwoods are more expensive and relatively difficult to work. Their high strength allows thin sections but this can effect stability, the wood tending to cup or twist. In use, hardwood can become polished and slippery, particularly when wet. Vacuum treated softwood is easily obtained, but the fluid used to treat the wood is toxic, presenting a potential hazard to people and animals. Cutting or drilling into softwood may also destroy the treatment, requiring repeat treatment once the deck is in place. The treatment fluid can also corrode metal fixings. If in doubt, seek specialist advice. In most situations, high strength and high durability softwood is the best option.

Timber decking provides a warm and easily laid surface for roof and basement gardens. The metal screws have become part of the ground pattern, and uplighters have been set into the stone chippings, which also allow drainage for the pot plants.

All countries publish durability ratings for different timber species and dimensioned timber converted from logs. These should be consulted or expert advice sought before any timber is purchased or specified. Generally moisture content should be below 15 per cent. Hardwoods tend to be stronger, more naturally durable and have a higher-quality appearance, but they are more expensive, more difficult to work with and can split, developing large and extremely sharp edges and splinters.

Decking timber, and timber generally, usually comes in standard lengths and it is sensible to design the overall dimensions of the deck so that there is minimal wastage. Most timber comes in lengths of 300 mm(1ft) increments. To allow for slight damage to the ends of boards it is wise to design the overall deck close to the standard length.

Remember that although the top surface of the deck will be exposed to the sun, drying winds and rain, the underside will remain shaded and dry. The uneven conditions tend to encourage cupping, prevented by using strong sections at a width to depth ratio of 2:1. The boards also need to be fixed firmly at their edges to underlying joists.

Structural advice

Decks need to be robustly constructed, with each element well supported, properly sized and connected. Cross bracing should be provided under high decks. To avoid danger of decking collapse, any load bearing needs to be transferred across or over the whole structure to avoid stress on a particular area.

For timber paths and where the deck sits directly on the ground, the principal is simply to support the deck boards, so that they provide an even flat surface. This will involve placing 25–50mm(1–2in)-thick joists or concrete bearers covered with timber battens on to a prepared surface so that the overall deck is level. The width of these need only be wide enough to accommodate fixings: 50mm(2in) will normally be sufficient. Inevitably, this will involve raising the ground level and the new level should be checked at the edges to see how the platform can be married into the surrounding levels. Uneven ground can be levelled by the addition of small pieces of wood, or shims, so that any bounce is eliminated. It will be a good idea to include a weed barrier or geotextile material over the soil, below the whole deck area which is then covered with decorative shingle or gravel. Adding a facia board around the edge of the deck may help to frame it and create a more finished look.

Decks built above ground level and on slopes will involve other key decisions. How high will the deck need to be? Will it involve more than one level? How big is it, and what shape? How wide does it need to be? Will it be stable, or might it move from side to side? How might it be fixed to a house? How might it work on a steep slope? Construction can be based on two or more layers of sub-structure. More layers will be simpler to construct, but end up with a deeper deck. The finished surface level and connections to surrounding surfaces and finishes may determine the depth of the deck structure and therefore its method of construction.

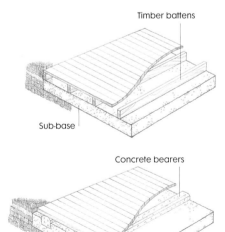

Timber battens

Sub-base

Concrete bearers

Sub-base

Two alternative methods of building decks directly on to the ground using timber battens and concrete bearers. Note that a weed barrier will be needed on top of the sub-base.

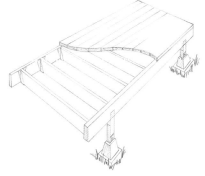

The two-layer (joist and deck board) system is slightly weaker, but shallower, allowing the surface to lie closer to ground or water level.

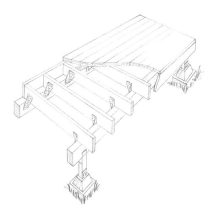

Three-layer (beam, joist and deck board) structures are simpler to construct as they require fewer joints.

When statutory approval will be required

➤ If the deck surface is 600mm(2ft) or more above ground level, building regulations normally require a balustrade of 1100mm(3ft7in). Although this is a safety precaution, an edge feature of some sort usually improves the appearance anyway. Local rules and codes should be checked.

➤ If the deck overlooks neighbours, or if the main building is in a conservation area, planning permission may be necessary.

➤ If the deck is at first floor or higher level, check planning and building regulations. It is wise to approach the local authority before they approach you! Ask for informal approval before proceeding too far with both the design and construction.

Choice of pattern and layout

Planning your deck is the most important part of the whole process. Care must be taken to arrive at the right decisions about aesthetics, proportions, colour, details, methods of joints and fixing, and choice of timber. The first stage will be to decide on the position, height, shape, length and surface pattern of the whole deck structure.

Timber staging is easily cut to follow various ground patterns. The raised edge projecting just proud of the slats and over the copper infill beneath marks the edge of the decking, and prevents wheelchairs and push-chairs from tipping over. Raised copper edging emphasizes the organic shape of the timber deck, and one natural material enhances the other.

Curved deck

Angled deck

Herringbone deck

Mitred deck

Diagonal deck

Some deck patterns require quite complex beam and joist arrangements to ensure that all deck boards are fully supported.

The overall layout and design should have a relationship with the immediate area especially if it is connected to a house and to allow areas for circulation, particularly close to doors and French windows.

If the deck is being used for outdoor eating with tables and chairs, it should be at least 3m(10ft) wide and preferably 4m(13ft), to allow people to move easily around when seated. If the deck is adjacent to a house, then locate it below the finished floor level so that water cannot collect adjacent to the house, where it might cause damage.

The deck boards are usually arranged across the direction of travel. Straight lines and rectilinear patterns are comparatively easy. The boards can be attached perpendicular to the joists, at an angle, diagonally, in herringbone or mitred patterns; and varying or alternating boards of different widths can achieve particularly effective patterns. Curved shapes, on the other hand, are much more difficult and may involve the boards having to be tapered, mitred, or skewed, which may, in turn, involve a lot of wastage. The joints, where the boards meet each other, will also be noticeable, and it will be worth considering the location of these in relation to the overall pattern. Joint locations can be random, alternating (rather like stretcher bond brickwork) or matched into straight lines (although to achieve this may involve more wastage). All boards should be laid with a 3–5mm($\frac{1}{20}$in) between them to allow for lateral movement (3 per cent across the width of the board throughout the season is the norm). This will result in a strong linear pattern, impacting on the finished appearance. Wider gaps can be a problem for children's fingers, high heels, and allow things to fall through.

To lengthen the appearance, lay your boards parallel to the viewing line; to widen it, lay the boards perpendicular to the view. Long parallel boards do show up any variations in joint width, but cross boarding at intervals helps break up this effect.

Changes in level

To fit with sloping ground, or to break up an otherwise large expanse of timber, changes of level can be designed into the deck. Platform levels can be separated by a single step that is usually the height of a single deck board laid on edge, which acts as a step riser. The top-level board should overlap to protect the riser board. This method of construction produces long steps that integrate fully with the surface patterns and can follow the overall patterns and shapes of the deck.

To connect levels further apart, or to join a higher deck with the surrounding ground, staircase construction should be used where treads and risers are fixed to stringers that form part of the sub-structure. Handrails will be needed for more than three steps. If ramps are required, then these should be constructed to recognized gradients (see Chapter 3) and grooved or non-slip deck boards used.

Timber footbridges

Small ponds or natural and artificial streams, can be greatly enhanced by the addition of crossings. It is possible to span quite large distances, using timber beams and deck boards. There are many manufacturers offering a range of catalogue products, available off the peg or with a bespoke design and consultancy service.

Bridges within gardens have a romantic quality and can form significant focal points. This was well known to garden designers of the eighteenth and nineteenth centuries and continues to be a central theme in oriental garden design. Famous small-scale bridges exist as images in Impressionist paintings – especially Monet's bridge at Giverny – in willow-pattern ceramics, in children's stories, where they might be a home to trolls or the focus of the game of Pooh sticks, and in film and TV dramas, where they might provide atmospheric meeting places.

Footbridges in gardens are a magnet for people who may wish to linger, especially if there is water flowing underneath. Handrails, therefore, become leaning posts, and it may be possible to peer through the gaps in the deck boards and watch the water flow underneath.

Worthwhile additions

Timber can be shaped, bevelled, routered and finished to enhance the overall quality and appearance of the structure without adding much to the overall cost. Lighting can be added to the underside of handrails or set on to the deck surface as uplighters. Trap doors can be set into the deck surface to allow access to useful storage space underneath, or even for children's play. Timber seats and storage boxes can also be built into the structure. Planters, sandpits and even hot tubs can be incorporated.

A shallow step gives prominence to this narrow bridge, with the wooden handrails allowing safe crossing and a place to lean over and view wild life. The simple design is in keeping with the rustic setting.

Through damp or boggy ground, raised walkways and bridges define the paths, keep feet dry and allow a clear passage. Occasionally wire netting is fixed over the slats to prevent slipping.

Remember, however, that additional structures (like moveable pots and barbecues) may impose a very significant extra permanent load and that substructures may need to be strengthened accordingly. Precautions should also be taken to ensure that areas below raised decks do not attract vermin.

Surface finishes and maintenance

Untreated timber, left outside, will eventually turn an attractive silver-grey colour that will harmonize with the surroundings and other furnishings as well as being easy and economical to maintain. Some modern translucent stains become patchy when worn and need stripping off to bare wood before being reapplied. Breathable organic products, such as natural oils, are best. Painted timber requires regular maintenance and the total length of timber in a typical deck should not be underestimated.

It is important to understand that timber naturally contains splits, cracks and knots, and that the appearance will alter with weather conditions. Regular checks will be needed for splinters and signs of damage or decay.

The main maintenance concern is usually to keep the decking clean and free from algae. Regular washing – especially shaded decks – with proprietary deck cleaners should keep the deck looking good and performing well, but do not use products that are damaging to plants or animals. Take care with pressure washers, as they have a tendency to raise the grain, which can turn into dangerous splinters. Never rub down a hardwood or cedar deck with steel wire wool or a wire brush or by the following day the deck will have turned black!

If metal furniture is to be used on the deck, cover the leg ends with rubber caps to prevent hollowing or iron stains.

❑ Decking is now established as a useful and attractive part of garden design and construction, but as it is often considered possible to build it cheaply, using inferior materials and fixings, it can be disappointing or look out of place. Provided you understand the location, use suitable materials and appreciate how they will interact, the possibilities for designing and using decking successfully are infinite.

Leading from the house to the woodland garden beyond, this light blue raised deck has been stained rather than painted for easier maintenance. The decorative wooden surround defines the edge and provides a safety barrier.

PRACTICALITIES

Calculating the size of timber

The sizing of timber components is the most complicated part of any deck design. There are a number of very useful publications, which are available from trade organizations and, nowadays, widely available on the Internet. For a large deck, above 10m²(100ft²), it will be advisable to consult a specialist designer or contractor, and for high decks, too, the advice of a structural engineer should also be sought.

The selection of the correct size of timber will not necessarily guarantee a strong and stable structure. The state of the ground, wind and exposure, patterns of use, strength of joints and fixings, and the quality of workmanship, may have a dramatic effect upon the overall stability of the deck. If any of these uses might pose a potential problem, then again, professional advice should be taken.

Timber sizes are based upon normally distributed loads. If, for example, the load is concentrated below a planter, then timber members will need to be closer together. The following section is advisory only.

Calculating the sizes of boards and joists	
Deck board size (mm)	Joist spacing (mm) i.e. span
21 x 88	450
35 x 70	500
35 x 95	650
35 x 120	660
35 x 145	660
40 x 100	600
45 x 70	830
45 x 95	960
45 x 145	990
Deck board size (in)*	Joist spacing (in)*
1 x 4 or 1 x 6	16
2 x 4 or 2 x 6	16
2 x 4 on edge	24
Decking board (1in board laid flat)	16
* NB Allowable spans for most commonly used decking in the USA.	

To calculate the overall length of timber needed in linear metres and feet:

Length of deck (mm) x width of deck (mm) ÷ (width of board + 3mm) ÷ 1000 = linear m

Length of deck (ft) x width of deck (ft) ÷ (width of board (ft) +.01(ft) = linear ft

A change of surface between staggered decking slats and cobbles, where drought-tolerant planting is used to enhance the composition and helps to blend the two different hard materials.

Calculating the size of deck boards

The key issue here is to balance the amount of material with the rigidity of the deck. The advantage of thicker boards is that they will span greater distances, however they will be more expensive. Thin boards will require a larger number of joists and need supporting underneath at closer intervals. Otherwise thin boards, not supported closely enough, will be springy and disconcerting.

The following table is for guidance only and is based upon using the most durable and the strongest type of softwood timber species.

Calculating the size of joists

The spacing between joists is determined by the thickness of the deck boards and the size of the joist timber. As a general rule, joist timber measuring 100x40mm (4inx2in) or 150x50mm(6inx2in) will need support from beams underneath no wider than 600mm(24in), although placing them on beams at 450mm(16in) spacings will make the deck less springy. It is best not to use timber thinner than 50mm(2in) thick, as it may split.

Where the depth of the joist timber is greater than four times its width, then blocking between the joists

Maximum Joist Span

Joist span i.e. beam spacing	Joist spacing (400mm or 450mm)	Joist spacing (600mm)
1.5m	100 x 50	150 x 50
2.0m	150 x 50	150 x 50
2.4m	150 x 50	200 x 50
3.0m	200 x 50	200 x 50
3.5m	200 x 50	250 x 50
3.6m	100 x 75	
4.9m	200 x 75	

Maximum Joist Span, USA

Joist span	Joist spacing (16in)	Joist spacing (24in)
2 x 6	7ft9in–9ft9in	6ft2in–7ft11in
2 x 8	10ft2in–12ft10in	8ft1in–10ft6in
2 x 10	13ft–16ft5in	10ft4in–13ft4in

Maximum Beam Spans

Span of bearer/beam i.e. post spacing	Span of joists		
	1.5m	2.0m	3.0m
1.3m	100 x 75mm	100 x 100mm	2 No 150 x 50mm
1.7m	2 No 150 x 50	2 No 150 x 50	2 No 150 x 50
2.0m	2 No 150 x 50	2 No 150 x 50	2 No 200 x 50

Maximum Beam Spans, USA

Spacing between beams	Beam size (in)	Maximum beam spans
48in	4 x 6	5ft10in–6ft
	3 x 8	7ft6in–8ft10in
	4 x 8	8ft2in–10ft
60in	4 x 6	5ft6in–5ft10in
	3 x 8	6ft8in–7ft6in
	4 x 8	8ft–9ft6in
72in	4 x 6	5ft2in–5ft6in
	3 x 8	6ft2in–7ft
	4 x 8	7ft9in–9ft
	4 x 6	3ft8in–4ft
	3 x 8	5ft10in–6ft6in
	4 x 8	7ft4in–8ft4in

NB As above, the range of beam spans allows for different types of wood. These are maximum values; it is acceptable for spans to be less.

should be included to prevent twisting. This is especially important if the edge joists are to have handrail supports attached to them.

Generally, two joist spacings are used, either 600mm (24in) or 450mm(16in). The table (below) also shows the recommended cross-sectional dimensions of the timber and assumes that this timber is vertical.

NB: The range of joist spacing allows for different types of wood. If stronger wood is used (Douglas fir, larch or southern pine), then the widest spacing can be applied. However, if weaker wood is used (cedar, balsam or white fir, other pines, spruce or redwood), then closer spacing will be needed. These are maximum values; it is acceptable for spans to be less than those listed.

Calculating the size of bearers/beams

It is quite common to support beams or bearers at a maximum of 2m(6ft) centres on to, or bolted to the sides of, posts. Sometimes it is difficult to purchase a single piece of timber of sufficient dimension and so often two thinner pieces are bolted together either side of the post; 50mm(2in)-thick timber is widely available.

Effective spans are calculated between supporting members rather than centre-to-centre.

Framing Method

Nearly all kinds of deck structure involve a number of layers of timber, where each layer is orientated perpendicular to the one above and below. This change of direction at each intersection of post/bearer/beam/joist/deck allows the timber to be fully supported and provides good fixing positions.

Where the platform needs to remain thin, because the finished surface level needs to be close to the ground, then it might be possible to adopt a two-layer system. This type of framing uses only bearers and deck

CONNECTING BEAMS

Metal fasteners

bolted or dowelled

Alternative ways of connecting beams to joists.

DIAGONAL BRACING

Diagonal bracing is important for above-ground structures and can be achieved in a variety of ways.

boards, but may require a large number of posts. A more common system is to adopt a three-layer approach – using beams, joists and deck boards – which require posts at approximately 2m(6ft) centres.

Planning the deck frame requires the surface deck patterns to have been designed along with the overall shape of the deck system, any changes in level, any features, such as planters or seats, and connections with ground level. A fundamental issue will be how to support all the ends of the deck boards. This will be particularly important, if the deck is curved or, if the deck boards are not located parallel to each other and perpendicular to the joists. Herringbone, angled, radial, and other patterns may require quite complex joist configurations to ensure that everything is fully supported and attached, especially at the ends.

Preventing movement

To prevent the whole deck moving from side to side, bracing and blocking may be required. Blocking involves placing short lengths of timber between the joists, to the full height, so that they cannot twist. It is particularly important if handrail supports are attached to the side of the joist, where leaning on the top of the support will twist it. Bracing involves the addition of diagonal timbers so that the structure becomes triangulated. Double diagonal, or cross bracing, is better still. Bracing will be important in deck systems higher than 1.5m(5ft).

All raised decks are attached to posts, which transmit the weight on to the foundation. Beams and bearers can sit on top of the post, or can be bolted to the side.

Joints, fixtures and fittings

To avoid the deck moving or developing a wobble at some time in the future, the joints must be rigid or the whole structure braced. Rigid joints using mechanical fixings (nails, screws, bolts, plate fixings) can work loose over time and it will be worth thinking about how to tighten them as a maintenance operation. The simplest means of attaching timber components together is to rest them one on top of the other and to attach simple metal brackets to stop them sliding from side to side. This will create quite a deep deck, and can look clumsy

in a small space. The depth can be significantly reduced by attaching timbers to the sides of other components or through the use of the housed or notched joints. To speed this process up, a number of simple frame connectors are available and include joist hangers, metal angles, steel straps, T- and L-shaped plates, post caps, post anchors, staircase anchors and metal post shoes and spikes.

Posts should ideally be fixed into hot dipped galvanized shoes or stirrups which are set into, or on to, concrete foundations. This allows the bottom of the post to remain above ground level where it will be less prone to rot or infestation. A gap of 25–75mm(1–3in) is recommended. Concrete pads, 150mm(6in) thick, can be used on solid, stable ground, and pre-cast concrete slabs, 65mm(approx 2½in) thick, can be used for small, low decks. Posts can also be driven or concreted into the ground where the below-ground part will assist in lateral support. In this case, the top surface of the concrete should slope away from the post to shed water.

Wallplates or ledgers are required where a deck meets a house or wall. These are sections of timber attached to the surface of the wall, which support the ends of the joists that rest on top of them (or to the side if a joist hanger is used). Standard wall fixing systems should be used, such as expanding bolts, shield anchors or, if the fixing is close to the edge of any masonry, injected adhesives.

When connecting beams on top of posts, they should be secured with post caps or T-shaped connectors. Two thinner beams can be bolted to the sides of posts so that the post is sandwiched between them.

Joists can be attached to the side of beams, using joist

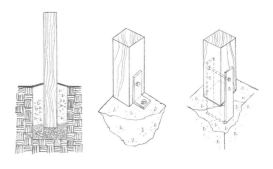

Alternative ground fixings for posts (see also page 145).

hangers, or can sit on top where they are held with a framing anchor. They can also be nailed at an angle to prevent sideways movement.

Deck boards should be fixed to joists, using two fixings at each intersection. Ideally holes for fixings should be pre-drilled, especially at the ends of the boards, where splitting is more likely to occur. Do not locate screws or nails closer than 12mm(¼in) to any edge. Screws are generally better than nails and gun nails can become loose. Do not countersink or punch fixings into the top surface as water can collect and cause rot. Nails should be driven in at an angle. Special deck screws, which do not need pre-drilled holes, are now widely available. Hidden fixings, which are driven into the sides of the boards create a neat finish, but are almost impossible to remove once fixed into place. This might be a problem if a deck board needs replacing.

All fixings should be hot dip galvanized, stainless steel, coated in baked epoxy, brass, or specially designed for long-lasting outdoor use. Do not use plain steel as it will rust and stain the timber. To attach deck boards and metal connectors it is best to use screws, although these can be time-consuming to fix. To attach substructure timber, such as beams to the sides of posts, it is best to use bolts, but nails may be appropriate if used to prevent timber slipping out of alignment. Lag bolts or coach screws (hex end) need pre-drilled holes and behave like large screws, requiring no nut. Carriage or coach bolts (rounded end) require holes to be drilled all the way through so that the bolts can be threaded through. Use 12mm(½in) bolts for larger frames and 10mm(⅜in) bolts for smaller framed systems. Bolts should be long enough to allow 5mm(¼in) to protrude beyond the nut with the inclusion of washers.

Handrails

Handrails and balustrades will be required at the edge of raised decks to prevent falls. They may also be required on lower decks and adjacent to ramped sections, where wheelchairs or buggies will be used. Regulations and legal codes vary around the world and these should be checked at the design stage. Handrails, located 1100mm (approx 30–40in) above deck level will both satisfy most

legal requirements and provide a comfortable height for anyone to lean on and place their drinks on.

Many of the design principles for fencing apply to handrails. One major difference is how the base of the supporting posts is connected. There are four main ways of doing this. The strongest is to extend a perimeter post through the deck to the heights of the handrail. Any leverage applied to the top of the post, by leaning for example, will be cancelled by the positive ground fixing. If this is not possible, or because it might look unattractive, the handrail supports can be bolted to the side of a perimeter joist or beam. This method is not as strong as the extended post version, as any sideways movement will cause the joist to twist. Blocking placed in between the joists will help to

In a fairly small space between prolific planting, raised decks and walkways allow close appreciation of the different species. Pots and other garden furniture define any unprotected edges.

Right **Bridge seats are required to support the ends of beams. Allow space for movement between the end of the bridge and the path.**

Handrails are normally attached to posts. Ideally they should be wide enough to stand objects on.

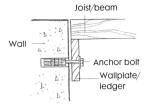

Joist/beam

Wall

Anchor bolt

Wallplate/ ledger

Fixing a ledger or wallplate to a wall can be achieved using a wall anchor bolt.

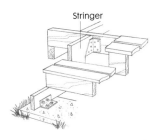

Stringer

A stepped stringer is used when connecting two layers of deck with timber steps. Note the use of metal connectors at the top and bottom.

prevent twisting. A much weaker version is to bolt the support post to a facia board or to the top of the deck boards, using a metal fixing plate.

The handrail itself should be free from splinters, and wide enough for people to lean on and ideally put down a wine glass. Fixings should be hidden and are best attached from underneath so that water cannot gather in screw holes or plugs. The space between the handrail and posts can be filled with vertical balusters, stretched material, such as canvas, glass or Plexiglas, tensile stainless steel cables (see also Practicalities, Chapter 7), or other means of preventing movement through the barrier. This is an important decision as, perhaps more than any other element of the deck, the handrail will affect its appearance. It will be worth looking at other examples, including boats and yachts, for clues and inspiration.

As in the case of fences, do not design or construct barriers that could be a hazard to children. A 100mm (4in) ball must be able to pass through all gaps, and horizontal rails should be avoided if small children are to use the deck where they can be used as a ladder.

Steps and changes in level

Where steps are required for access to or from a deck, or to move from one level to another, they should be incorporated into the overall design at the layout planning stage. The easiest way to add steps is through the addition of stepped stringers which act rather like joists, but which are cut to receive timber treads.

The size of treads and risers will be determined by the height of the level change and the distance of travel, but, where possible, you should use whole widths of timber to avoid cutting or using unnecessarily complicated joints. For example, two 140mm(6in nominal – 5½in actual)-wide boards and a 3mm (¼in)-gap can be used to make a tread 283mm(11¼in) wide. Three boards will make a tread 426mm(17in) wide. The same boards set on edge with an overhanging horizontal tread board of 25mm(2in nominal – 1½in actual) thickness above will make a riser 165mm(7in) high.

Steps may require handrails which should be located approximately 900mm(approx 35in) above the pitch line (see Chapter 3 for detail on steps).

Simple timber footbridges

Many of these principles can be applied to short and simple timber footbridges. There are a number of special requirements that bridges have which will need to be considered. All, or nearly all footbridges, will need handrails or barriers. Beams or spanning devices will require bearings at each end.

The simplest form of spanning device is a beam and these can be used for bridges, up to about 6m(approx 19½ft) long. In most garden situations, low cost timber logs are used and are useful for straight crossings. Steel beams can span wide distances, and can be fabricated into curves The span distance and loading requirements will determine the species of wood used and method of construction. Particularly suitable species are Douglas fir, European redwood, western hemlock and larch. Like large decks, footbridges are specialist structures, and professional advice should be sought before embarking on a complex or possibly expensive construction.

The design of deck boards, handrails and methods of jointing and fixing will be the same as for decks. One significant difference will be the requirements for bearings to support the end of the beam. These are normally constructed from concrete but could also be made from large section timber or even wire gabions. The bearing has two functions. The first is to support the beam, and a gap should be left between the end of the beam to allow for expansion of the timber. The second function of the bearing is to act as an edge to the path, which connects to the bridge. The beam can be attached to the concrete with metal angles, but bolt holes should be slotted rather than circular so that the timber can move freely from side to side as it expands and contracts. Because the footbridge acts as an extension to the path or circulation network within the garden, the width dimensions should meet the same criteria as described in Chapter 2. Design should keep the underside of the beam away from the bearing so that water does not collect and cause rot.

Unlike decks, timber footbridges are usually made from just two layers: beams and deck boards. If deck boards with dimensions 150x50mm(2x6in) are used and screwed or nailed directly on to the top of the beams, then the number of beams required can be taken from the table below. Bear in mind that the larger dimensions shown in the table represent nearly a whole tree and will be very difficult (and expensive) to source.

Steel beams can span very wide gaps, but provide a complication where timber needs to be fixed to metal. However, their greatest advantage in garden design is their ability to allow subtle curves to be introduced, but this adds the complication of having to cut deck boards to accommodate the curved shape.

Beam sizes for decks

Beam size (mm)	900mm-wide deck		1200mm-wide deck	
	No of beams	Span	No of beams	Span
150 x 75	3	3.0m	3	2.75m
200 x 100	3	4.5m	3	4.0m
250 x 150	3	6.5m	3	5.75m
250 x 200	2	6.25m	3	7.5m
300 x 225	2	7.25m	3	8.0m
350 x 250	2	9.3m	3	9.6m

US Conversion

Beam size (in)	3ft-wide deck		4ft-wide deck	
	No of beams	Span	No of beams	Span
3 x 6	3	10ft	3	9ft
4 x 8	3	15ft	3	12ft
6 x 10	3	21ft	3	18½ft
8 x 10	2	20ft	3	24½ft
7 x 12	2	24ft	3	26ft
8 x 14	2	30ft	3	31½ft

Doubling as a jetty, a simple staggered walkway is reflected in the water below. The upright timber posts driven into the mud below are also useful for tying up boats. Reflection in water is always an added bonus.

Outside a timber-clad building, decking of the same species is used to produce a unified composition.

Varying the edge of a ground-level deck creates the opportunity for a range of planting bed sizes and helps to break up the hard lines.

Roughly cut boards project over the pond but are unsafe to walk on. The useable area is defined by a simple string line.

Placed at strategic points to break up the length of the path, these timber planks are set at right angles to the others.

Clean simple lines and a strong shadow line create a sharp contrast between deck and water. A dark lining for the pool is important.

Children love this sculptural effect created by 'stepping stones' of triangular decking panels, inviting them to cross the water.

These timber boards sit on a floating raft which can rise and fall with water levels.

The combination of timber and galvanized steel framed by timber edges makes a strong architectural pattern.

Timber decking principles can be used sculpturally. This composition is enhanced by the direct transition between straight lines, curves and platforms.

The combination of a brushed steel handrail and large section timber makes a strong contrast. Note the edge and bolt detail.

Simple lines and traditional detailing combine to create a relaxing waterside platform which is generous enough to allow a variety of uses.

Decks need not be laid in parallel lines. Varying the pattern creates added variety.

The irregular arrangement of the supporting posts, the outward jutting timbers and an irregular handrail make a strong design statement in a rural location.

Across a shallow dry streambed, where safety is not a problem, the solid timber beams are separated and held in an arch by spaced timber pegs.

Well suited to rocky or coastal areas, this timber walkway gives access to land that might otherwise be inpenetrable .

Woven rails and sawn timbers fit well with the woodland setting where a heavier structure could easily look out of place.

Strong architectural lines, steps and changes in level, cast strong shadows in this bold geometric design.

Depending on the location, bridge handrails can be intricate or simple, but must be sturdy. Here off-cuts have been pieced together to make a strong pattern.

GARDEN STRUCTURES & FURNISHINGS

Garden structures, such as arches or pergolas, can create perfect private settings for relaxation, quiet contemplation or togetherness. Whether in town or country, most gardens need some structural features to provide for modern outdoor living. As well as being functional or decorative, these features give a vital architectural element to a garden; they define spaces, give height, provide an overhead plane, act as focal points, or support plants. Historically garden structures illustrate an extensive range of ideas and styles, ranging from Doric and neo-Palladian temples, Gothic loggias and sham castles, through to modernist pavilions and sculptural follies, such structures often becoming the dominant focus of the garden.

Although most gardens will not require such extravagances, the inclusion of some simple structures can offer the advantages of:

- providing shade and shelter for relaxation and entertaining
- providing a covered link between house, terrace and garden
- framing a view leading to a focal point
- providing support for climbing plants
- creating a focal point or gathering space
- giving some vertical architecture to the garden
- introducing sculptural, but practical elements
- providing an opportunity to use a wider variety of materials

GENERAL GLOSSARY OF COMPONENTS FOUND IN GARDEN STRUCTURES

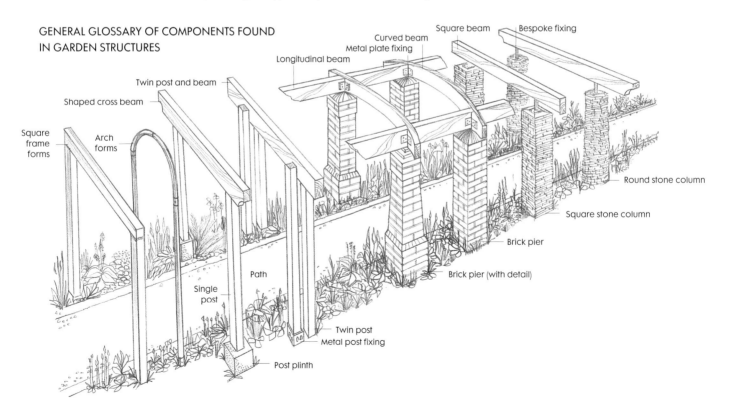

Key design questions

▸ Where might the structure be best located to provide a focus, to frame a view, create an enclosure, extend a living/entertaining area or provide shade? Have all design opportunities been fully considered and exploited?

▸ What is the most appropriate choice of material or materials for the design context, style and locality?

▸ Will the structure be comfortable to use and will the height and shape allow easy access?

▸ Will the structure be strong enough to support plants when fully grown and full of foliage?

▸ Can the structure be maintained when covered with vegetation?

▸ What is the expected design life of the structure? Can individual components be replaced if they fail early?

▸ Will the ground fixing positions compromise the volume of soil required for healthy plant growth? Will they be strong enough to prevent the structure being pushed over by the wind, especially if covered with vegetation?

▸ Is the structure fully braced or will the joints be rigid enough to prevent twisting or moving out of shape?

▸ Have you checked that your 'bespoke design' is not already available ready-made, where it might be cheaper and easier to construct?

▸ Most structures are climbable. Is yours safe for children, especially if they fall?

Structures provide the opportunity for a covering link between house and garden. Here various changes in level are linked by bold timber uprights, painted to set off the planting and to co-ordinate with furniture and furnishings.

Most simple structures affect the way in which a garden is used. Some can be located to generate mystery, anticipation and surprise. Tunnels, for example, can move you quickly from light through darkness or filtered sunlight, before bursting out again into light. An arch is quickly negotiated, while a pergola allows you to absorb, at a leisurely pace, views of the garden or surrounding landscape. All these closely-related features are also used to give vertical accents to the garden, whether for shelter, shade or privacy.

A pergola is a covered walkway, normally consisting of a double row of posts or pillars, which support cross beams. Some pergolas may be attached to a wall or building on one side to form a shelter or, if covered overhead, a loggia. Pergolas were originally structured for the support of vines and climbing fruit trees; they later developed into intricate covered walkways to provide shade in Renaissance gardens. More recently a pergola has become an architectural element, often linking the horizontal plane of the terrace near the house to other areas of the garden by a sheltered paved walkway with brick, stone, metal or timber supporting posts and piers, each linked by cross beams of timber or metal. The piers are a method of displaying climbing roses, wisteria, clematis, honeysuckle or other desirable climbers.

An arcade is a series of arches and a colonnade is a row of columns, many of these easily being confused with pergolas, but for the purist or garden historian, the terminology should be correct.

An arbour is a freestanding shelter, most often covered in climbing plants. Some are made entirely from living trees and shrubs trained into dome-like forms. Others have developed from trellis and tent-like canopies used since the Middle Ages to allow people to enjoy the delights of a garden, out of the direct rays of the sun.

A gazebo or summerhouse is a small garden room, or 'look-out', with a roof and a view. Most are placed at a strategic point within a garden, so that they can be seen as a key focal point.

Climbing plants need some support to set them off, and to help them climb. If spaced further apart, the uprights of this rustic pergola would give people more room to pass through.

Design considerations in choosing garden structures

Pergolas and arches

An initial decision is whether to take your lead from the style and materials of the house and the design of the garden, or to purposefully contrast these with something different. In either case the two should be compatible. The structure will contribute to the overall composition of the garden and be seen in relation to the house as well as from within it. Pergolas or arches should draw you positively through the space in a given direction or act as an edge, helping to define a space. Remember that, unless the plants designed to clothe the pergola are evergreen, the bare structure will be evident for much of the year.

In keeping with a more classic style of architecture, this pergola draws one through the space, with deciduous climbing wisteria providing shade.

▸ Pergolas can enhance the status of a path and make right-angled turns more meaningful. The overall proportions are crucial; the construction should be sturdy. Lightweight pergolas can collapse under the weight of plants, but an overly heavy-weight structure can appear too dominant.

▸ The closer the spacing or span of the crossbeams straddling the walkway beneath, the greater the sense of overhead enclosure.

▸ The degree of shade will be affected by both the density of the climbing plants, and also by the spacing of the horizontal or overhead beams.

▸ Ensure even spacing between uprights along the whole length of the structure.

▸ The width should generally be greater than the height. Additional width might be required if vigorous or arching plants are grown at the sides.

▸ Successful heights for uprights or piers should be anything from 2.2m–2.45m (7–8ft) above ground level, 2.45–2.75m(8–9ft) wide, and with columns 2.75–3.65m (9–12ft) apart, along the length.

▸ If the surface level of the path beneath steps up, the pergola must step up accordingly. On slopes, any longitudinal beams can run parallel to the ground.

▸ A break in the pergola, possibly missing out a couple of uprights, can avoid a tunnel-like appearance and create welcome relief from continuous shade.

▸ Carefully-orientated horizontal components need not prohibit sunlight.

▸ Use an enticing focal point, such as a seat or an urn, to tempt you on through the structure to the end.

The surface level beneath this pergola steps up. The height of the pergola uprights allows for this change, with longitudinal beams running parallel to the ground and 'ladder cross beams' supporting the weight of vines.

Standard width

Wide planting within columns

Enclosed living willow arbour

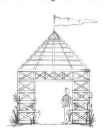

Social gathering space

Tall, thin, arched roof

Tall thin

Tunnel

Cross-sections showing proportions of height and width to a person. Some feel more intimate than others.

A tempting 'surprise' element in a country setting. The surrounding trees show off the curved roof line, while climbing plants add to the romantic effect. Regular clearance of encroaching vegetation may be needed to maintain the view through to the landscape beyond.

Arbours

Many types of structure qualify as arbours – they can be grand, simple, rustic (even ruined), sculptural or architectural. Styles can be traditional or contemporary, generously detailed or minimalist. Global styles and traditions can also be observed and exploited successfully where appropriate. Although the main function of an arbour is to provide a static, shady retreat, arbours also give vertical definition to the space and therefore their positioning is crucial. Their appearance should be tempting and inviting. Usually they are placed at a distance, either as a focal point or to provide a tantalizing glimpse of an intriguing feature; arbours can also act as a 'full stop' to a part of the garden. Remember that the roof line of the arbour will be seen against surrounding trees or buildings, and the structure can be softened if surrounded by scented climbing or border plants, adding to the romantic effect.

Metal arbours are visually lighter and more elegant than those made of timber – if they are painted black, they are virtually invisible from a distance, especially if placed against a backdrop of trees or other vegetation. Many fine examples still exist in historic gardens, and it is worth seeking them out to imitate or to inspire you. Good wrought iron arbours can still be obtained, but generally they are made to order by skilled blacksmiths. Ready-made products tend to be small, flimsy, and lack the craftsmanship that distinguishes the quality product from the mass-produced. You can adapt manufacturers' examples as a basis for your own design, and those using powder-coated metal are colourful and long lasting.

Timber arbours tend to look heavy, although, if properly detailed, they can be beautiful architectural additions to larger gardens. Many designs are widely available, often at great expense, and designed to fit into a wide range of situations, although not especially effective in any. If the budget allows, it is worth having a bespoke arbour designed and constructed. But it will be important to try to visualize any new addition and its relationship with other elements before making an expensive purchase. As the prime purpose of an arbour is to provide a shaded sitting area, remember that the floor area needs to be large enough to house a table and chairs, or built-in furniture, and to allow people to circulate. A minimum of 3–4m (9ft9in–13ft) in any one direction should be considered.

Bundles of stems have been used to form arches with additional material feathered in as the sides near the ground.

Arches

These are strong vertical elements, often forming important punctuation points, gateways, thresholds and elements of surprise. To successfully integrate into your garden, they must be planned as part of the design. They work best as apertures in walls or fences where they are used as a point of emphasis, either to draw attention to an entrance, to frame views, or to link divided areas. Individual free-standing arches marooned in a sea of lawn serve no purpose at all, and growing plants up them only draws attention to a design mistake.

Gazebos and summerhouses

As forms of simple or complex garden structures, gazebos, summerhouses and grottoes can have an important impact on a garden. Rather like arbours, they are secluded and romantic places from which to enjoy the view. Although most are

Siting any garden building needs careful consideration. The structure may either create a feature, a focal point, or it may be a destination. The base of this summerhouse has been built out into the water to give a better view of the surroundings.

Not only for children, tree houses can also provide alternative office space. A good local carpenter can sometimes design and build a more interesting and unusual structure than is available commercially.

bought readymade, sources of inspiration can come from Japanese teahouses through to thatched huts from the South Seas, Eccentricity is always an endearing trait in garden buildings, and a little research into books on old gardens may help you visualize an original addition to your garden architecture.

Tree houses or play equipment

Much is now commercially available, usually at either great expense or in dubious primary colours (often made from plastic) that can become the main focal point in a garden although the treehouse itself might only be used a few days a year. It is usually less expensive and far more interesting to create your own. Treehouses are not just the exclusive preserve of children, and have recently been developed as alternative office

space, health sanctuaries, or to fulfil other needs for quiet space. The first requirement is a sturdy tree with strong, well-spaced branches. If access for children if difficult, a rope ladder will afford more privacy and enjoyment.

The main ingredients are an access ladder or staircase, plus a wooden floor surrounded by wooden panels, often with windows or gaps for enjoying views from the higher level. Commercial firms now command high prices for supplying various kits to include swings, rope nets, ladders and other challenging forms of children's play activities. Construction is similar to that of most garden buildings, so a local carpenter may just as easily be able to work to your design. Timber is the obvious material, and hardwoods, such as oak, will endure for longer than pressure-treated softwood.

All timber should be planed or free from splinters. Where children may play unsupervised (part of the fun of a tree house), safety is a prime factor and, unless you are confident about your work, the help of a professional designer or manufacturer might be a worthwhile investment.

The increasing popularity of water features has led to the occasional incorporation of small- or large-scale grottoes, built from various materials such as fossils, tufa, pebbles or glass.

Grottoes

Originally the prerogative of the rich, grottoes were first inspired by European examples, encountered by the elite on the Grand Tour. Walls were lined with shells brought from exotic shores and arranged to simulate natural caverns, dug into earth or rock and earthed over. Chilly, gloomy and sometimes frightening places, but often favourites with children, grottoes are still being built today. Specialist designers can provide them as large- or small-scale structures, complete with fossils, coral, bones, lumps of diseased wood, pebbles, glass and tufa. Grottoes are now sometimes also used as an interesting backdrop to water features. Not difficult to construct, successful grottoes do require rich imagination and a variety of materials.

Fabric structures

Those extending from a house or wall tend to be known as awnings and provide protection from wind or variable weather conditions. They can either be reeled out or stretched over a framework of overhead beams. Freestanding fabric structures tend to be based on two main design precedents: tents and sails. Tent-like structures are suspended and stretched from timber or metal poles and held in place with guy ropes attached to pegs in the ground or eyelets in walls or from other surrounding fixtures. Fabric can be waterproof canvas, polyesters or other proprietary materials. Very lightweight material tends to flap around in the wind and become noisy. A sophisticated touch is achieved by matching the colour or pattern to the interior design of your house, plain colours usually being the most successful, and pale fabrics can contrast with darker paintwork. Avoid white, as it can be rather glaring in strong sun and is easily marked. Colourful patterned or striped materials can give an oriental or Middle Eastern effect. For a party, try using thin muslin to filter the sun and create a magical shady place.

Some companies provide a bespoke design and manufacturing service. Marine and sail manufacturers have recently branched into the garden equipment and architecture market, making some beautiful and elegant canopy structures. Marine technology is very advanced and components are beautifully made, a pleasure to use, surprisingly cheap and long lasting. Because the structures are permanently in tension, they make very little noise. They can also be designed to be de-mountable or to fold, so they can be stored during the winter, and easily cleaned.

A word of caution…

❑ Many a garden design layout has been spoilt by the purchase and inclusion (or obstinate retention) of a useful, ready-made shed or greenhouse. These necessary items are best collected in a 'working area' ideally separated from the rest of the garden by a hedge, fence or wall.

Advanced marine technology has now extended into making garden canopies. Sturdy and long lasting, these sail-like canopies are held in permanent tension, creating very little noise.

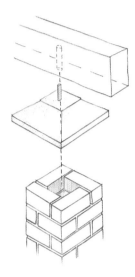

PRACTICALITIES

Masonary columns require a cap or coping to shed water. Careful detailing is needed to secure the beam to the top, but a simple metal pin is all that is required.

MASONRY AND STONE COLUMNS

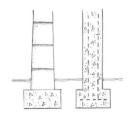

Brick   Rubble stone

Dressed   Reinforced
stone/Ashlar   concrete

Plan ahead

The key consideration is to plan ahead, co-ordinating the work so that any heavy machinery – used for digging wall footings or paving foundations – also carries out any excavations for the proposed structures whilst still on site. Planning ahead will save money and also avoid later damage to the established garden. Cable runs for lighting, water and electric pumps will also need to be considered at the planning stage.

Principles of garden structures

It is no accident that structures throughout the world and throughout history tend to look similar – at least structurally. This is because the laws of physics limit the size and shape of structures, especially the relationship between the strength of materials and their ability to support their own weight. It is therefore not always possible to design structures based only on aesthetic principles of proportion, although technological advances in structural engineering and materials now allow many seemingly bizarre structures to be realized.

Basic rules should be observed – upright elements, such as posts and columns, should be vertical so that they support their own weight. Heavy columns will need a foundation to prevent them sinking into the ground.

Horizontal elements should be sufficiently strong or deep not to bend or sag under their own weight or under the additional weight of plants. Decorative rope or chain swags are an exception. Adding a curve to a horizontal beam, so that it resembles a shallow arch, will improve its strength dramatically. Downward forces on horizontal members will have a tendency to pull the posts or columns inwards and so some bracing may be required if the posts are slender.

Because garden structures tend to be lightweight and not to be constructed like buildings with significant downward loads, they must be built to withstand strong lateral forces, such as high winds, acting upon their sides.

These forces most strongly effect the parts of the structure where components meet in joints or fixings. Therefore, it is the connections that need to be considered and detailed. These should be strong and rigid enough to prevent the whole structure rotating or sliding away from the vertical. In timber this is achieved by using cut joints or mechanical fixings; in metal by using welded, brazed joints, or by fixing bolts or rivets.

In order to help structures remain vertical, lateral support can be provided in three ways. First, by making the joints very rigid. Second, by providing diagonal bracing. Third, by adding sheet material that is attached all around the frame. Plywood, timber panels, sheet metal and even concrete can be attached to posts or columns, wrapping a structure to prevent twisting and lateral movement. With all methods it is important that lateral support is arranged in a fairly symmetrical fashion.

Working with materials

Choice of materials is diverse and should be appropriate to the context. The permanence and speed or ease of construction may also be a deciding factor; for instance a brick and stone arch will involve specialist skill while a ready-made iron or steel frame, or even a woven structure can perhaps be bought at a country fair or from a mail order company and erected immediately. Usually these woven structures are flimsy and it is wise to remove them under cover during winter months.

Treated softwood timber structures will last for about 25 years or so, but will start to look tired after 15 years. Hardwood structures can last for many years – at least 40 if well maintained. Timber has an added advantage that it is more easily worked by amateurs, although the skill required to achieve accurate joints or high-quality detailing in hardwoods should not be under-estimated. Working with metal requires skill and practice and is usually best left to professionals.

Masonry columns and piers

Traditionally, pergola uprights or piers in large gardens would have been made from brick or stone, which was strong enough to support sturdy timber cross beams. Hollow brick columns should be a minimum of one-and-

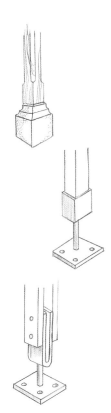

a-half bricks square (327.5x327.5mm[1ft1inx1ft1in]), but piers of 675x675mm(approx2ftx2ft), and even 900x 900 mm(3ftx3ft) can also be used. More commonly a hollow box section, approximately 450x450mm(1ft6inx1ft6in) is built surrounding four reinforcing rods that have been cast into a concrete foundation. The central cavity is then backfilled with wet concrete to form a solid reinforced concrete pier with brick facing. Many different types of brick are available and, by varying the size, colour and profile of the pier edges, different patterns are possible.

Stone columns are based around traditional walling methods. Finely-dressed or ashlar stone will produce an exceptionally high-quality finish, but at considerable cost. Rubble stone will need to be mortared together, usually around a reinforced concrete or metal core, so that the stone is decorative rather than structural. Drystone piers need to be very carefully constructed, as tall drystone columns are extremely vulnerable to movement and subsequent collapse. They are not recommended. Dimensions are less critical than for bricks, and decisions will be based on overall proportions, not on structural requirements. Traditional stone columns made from large sections, one above the other, are made to order and will be very stable if correctly constructed on a concrete foundation that should extend 100mm(4in) beyond the edge of the column bay and be at least 450mm(1ft6in) deep. Reconstituted stone columns are widely available, usually in classical designs, but increasingly in more contemporary styles. Manufacturers provide detailed guidance for their construction. In order to build a stone pier or column from smaller units mortared together, dimensions should rarely be less than 450mm(1ft6in) wide.

Cast concrete columns can be used and carefully profiled and detailed using well designed formwork and high-quality workmanship. Columns can be quite slender, even 150mm(6in) in diameter, but will need to be reinforced; and the concrete should be very carefully specified. Using concrete affords almost unlimited possibilities for the overall shape, and also provides occasion for clever detailing of connections to other components.

Tapered masonry columns are more interesting than straight-sided versions and produce a more attractive connection between vertical and horizontal members. But they are only really possible with stone or concrete.

Caps, copings and finials at the tops of masonry columns need careful thought and can also be one of the most significant parts of the whole design. The principles are that they should protect the top of the column from water penetration, and ideally project outwards so that water is shed away from the sides. The basic design principle provides many opportunities for including decorative shapes and mouldings and also for playing with overall proportions. Beautifully dressed stone, or accurately cast, reconstituted stone, juxtaposed with rough, rubble walling stone, is a particularly successful combination. Classical capitals, based upon Greek or Roman architectural orders can be purchased, but in general, simple styles with clean lines are best.

Caps and copings should be located on a metal pin, which has been cast into the top of the column, to prevent the comparatively lightweight unit becoming dislodged. If any joints are present in the top detail, a damp-proof membrane should be used immediately under the cap or coping stone.

A bold design statement can be achieved by adding to the top of the column a decorative finial or ornament made from stone, ceramic, metal or other material, especially at the ends of structures, at corners and changes of direction. These can be purchased, made, found or commissioned.

Vertical timber components

Timber is now the most frequently used material for making both vertical and horizontal sections and is the easiest to handle. Styles vary enormously, from basic structures with two uprights and a cross beam to other designs using complex joints, curved or bent sections, decorative panels, trellis and detailed patterning.

Rustic timber, normally larch poles, can be simply nailed or lashed together and work well in an informal setting. But the bark soon falls off and the timber rots within a few years.

Beam size	Span
225x50mm(9x2in)	4.0m(13ft)
200x50mm(8x2in)	
3.8m(12ft.6in)	
125x50mm(5x2in)	2.5m (8ft2in)
125x50mm(5x2in)	1.8m(6ft)

It is useful to keep the bottom of timber posts clear of the ground by using bespoke metal supports or by sitting the posts on a decorative stone plinth. (See also page 126.)

JOINTS AND CONNECTIONS

Timber post and canopy with metal pin connector

Hollow metal section, welded joints

Hollow metal section, mechanical joints

Metal can be jointed using welded or braced joists, or by mechanical fixings and special connectors. Special details are needed for combining metal and timber.

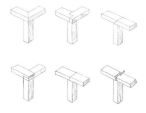

Joints suitable for attaching horizontal members to the tops of posts.

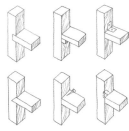

Joints used for connecting to the sides of posts.

For a more permanent structure, treated softwood or hardwood should be used. Choice of timber will depend upon appearance, durability, expected life span of the structure, and the availability and skill of the person undertaking the construction. Hardwoods, such as oak, are expensive but will last for many years. Naturally durable softwoods are also a good option.

All timber used outdoors is most vulnerable at the point where it meets the ground. Freestanding timber structures are comparatively heavy and tend to stay where they are put. Ground fixings are therefore required to keep them in place and prevent them from being pushed sideways or blown away. Posts are usually set into the ground between 500mm(1ft6in) and 750mm(2ft6in) deep and backfilled with rammed earth or concrete. Attractive details can be achieved using metal fixings, which separate the post from the ground. Alternatively, metal shoes can be used. High-quality ground details can also be achieved by setting the post on to a stone, concrete or metal plinth. Stone plinths were commonly used in oak and other timber framed buildings to separate timbers from the ground.

As a minimum, 100mm(4in)-posts should be used, with 125mm(5in)-posts being slightly more generous and larger-section posts making a grander statement, enhancing the possibilities of experimenting with overall proportions. Columns that look particularly attractive with climbers can be made using four 75mm(3in) section posts, set 400–450mm(8–10in) apart to form a square box section to which vertical, horizontal or diagonal battens can be attached rather like trellis.

Metal structures

Metal will absorb heat, which in warmer countries may affect plant growth. Plastic-coated tubular metal avoids this, but the plastic coating is unattractive in comparison with other finishes, such as powder coating, galvanized metal or paint. Uprights need to be firmly bedded into soil, or concreted into position.

Steel structures tend to be made from solid rods or extruded sections, which are welded together. Solid rods should be between 12.5mm($\frac{1}{2}$in) and 25mm(1in) diameter. The tube section should be 35–75mm(1–2in)

and the joints must be rigid to make a strong frame. These rigid joints are best achieved through welded junctions, but mechanical fixings, such as bolts, rivets and carefully detailed flush screw fixings, are also possible, with the added advantage that the structure can be delivered flat for assembly on site.

Elegant metal arches can be bent to create generous wide tunnels used to train fruit trees, vines and climbers. Uprights should be buried 300mm(12in) deep and concreted in, unless planting is close to the support,

Horizontal components

Most garden structures use timber beams to create the horizontal roof plane.

Timber beams should be at least 150mm(6in) deep and a minimum of 50mm(2in) thick; but a measure of 175–225mm(7–9in) will look and feel more generous. It is worth experimenting with proportions. Lightweight beams on heavy, thick columns will look odd, as will heavy, deep beams between flimsy lightweight posts.

Connecting a timber cross beam to a timber post can be done in a number of ways. The simplest is to bolt or screw the beam to the side of the post. This works especially well if the post is sandwiched between two beams. By cutting a rebate into the side of the post to create a halving joint, a more elegant joint can be achieved and some of the weight of the beam will be carried more directly down through the post, putting less pressure on the fixing. Cutting notches and rebates on to both vertical and horizontal components provides a wide variety of structural and decorative possibilities, and further allows more than two pieces of timber to meet at the same place, and at the same level. A variety of ways of jointing timber are illustrated here.

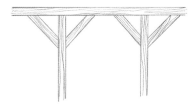

Taller and lightweight structures may need diagonal bracing to prevent twisting, especially in exposed areas.

Cross beams will often project beyond the line of the uprights and can be cut and detailed to create patterns and shapes. Many have oriental references, but numerous shapes are possible.

The tops of all horizontal components should be cut or angled slightly to shed water.

Timber can also be connected to brick, stone and metal columns by using specially designed components, although very few of these are available off-the-peg. If specially commissioned, this type of connection provides an opportunity for a special detail.

Side beams, which run parallel to the paths or along the structure, can be used to provide a framework for metal or wire cross-members, which are especially suited to training climbing plants. Metal rods and tubes can be used with the advantage that they put little or no strain on the framework structure. Copper or stainless tubing can be bent into arches and flattened at junctions and ends so that it can be drilled and bolted together and to posts. Strained wire and braided stainless steel cable can be used to great effect, but need a rigid metal frame, and the wires tightened, putting the whole structure into significant tension.

Horizontal frames will require carefully detailed connections to posts and columns.

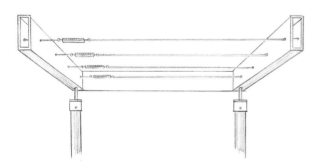

Strained wire puts structures under a great deal of tension and is best used for metal frames.

Lightweight timber and metal can be combined into box-like beams that are continuously braced into girder-like sections, creating a three-dimensional framework. The rigidity of the joints will be critical to the strength of the whole structure. Where possible, welded rather than mechanical connections should be used.

Fixing pergolas to walls and buildings

There are two main ways to attach overhead beams to side walls, both of which are discussed in detail in Chapter 6. The first is to attach a wall plate or ledger of 100x50mm(4inx2in) to the wall on which the beams sit. The second method is to fix joist hangers at fixed intervals to the wall. An attractive and durable detail can be achieved above door openings and French windows by adding a 450mm(1ft6in)-board to the tops of the beams where they meet the wall, and covering it with lead or roofing felt. A flashing strip that covers the gap between the wall and the roof section will be needed and the whole detail must slope away from the house.

Working with plants

If posts and columns are to have plants grown alongside the base, then the ground position should be detailed to ensure sufficient soil and stability to provide optimum conditions for plant growth. This may mean varying the amount and location of concrete foundations, perhaps favouring metal shoe fixings or rammed earth for timber and metal structures. Do not compromise foundations under stone and brick columns.

Plants can be trained unobtrusively by threading wires through metal eyes screwed into the uprights and cross-beams. Softwoods can either be left to weather naturally, or be stained or painted. Plants need to be chosen carefully so that they do not swamp lighter frames.

Woven stems

Flexible, informal yet short-lived garden structures can be constructed from woven stems of hazel, willow, split bamboo or any other material that will last at least one growing season. These are useful for providing a quick fix support for climbing plants, such as runner beans or sweet peas, but unless securely anchored by bent wire pegs threaded through the lower weave, they can easily be blown away.

Freshly planted willow stems, creating a pattern of dappled shade, can also be used to create tunnels, their arching stems being sufficiently pliable to make it possible to follow the curve of a path.

WALL FIXING

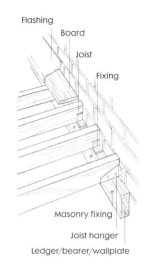

Flashing
Board
Joist
Fixing
Masonry fixing
Joist hanger
Ledger/bearer/wallplate

Timber ledgers and bearers allow structures to be bolted to walls. The point of connections can collect water and so needs special detailing.

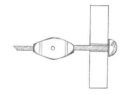

Tightening devices must be incorporated in strained wire or cable runs.

Transluscent plastic sheet catches the light and can be attached to frames to make outdoor screens. Doors and window apertures can be easily incorporated.

The outline and diagonal design of the wooden arbour is complemented in the shape of the metal seat, the colour of paint unifying both highly decorative items.

The timber uprights and the roof of this garden building are stained in a dull blue, providing a subtle finish requiring less regular maintenance than paint.

Highly fashionable in nineteenth-century Italian gardens, water features and grottoes were both a technological innovation and a source of amusement.

The understated simplicity of adjustable shutters and blinds in this timber-framed building contrast with the manicured planting of the Japanese style garden.

In a woodland environment, a minimalist metal and timber structure uses gabions infilled with logs as seating and space dividers. Tensile wires are stretched will support plant growth.

As a support and foil for climbing plants, copper arbours need no maintenance, and blend well with other natural materials such as timber and brick.

Complementary in both style and colouring, the planting surrounding this gazebo helps integrate it into the surroundings.

Clear plastic bent-over metal arches provide an amusing and colourful addition, although it is likely to be short-lived.

White wisteria cascades from square stone columns, supporting a wide span of heavy timber beams. Note the corbel supports and the wide joist spacing.

Set into a wooden fence, this curved arbour provides a pleasant place to relax and breaks up the fence line. If neither varnished nor painted, the hardwood timber weathers to a natural silvery-grey colour.

A curved bamboo blind sitting on a supporting steel girder, reduces the glare from the pale stonewalls of this courtyard.

Metal arches or hoops can be combined to create tunnels which act as a frame to support a variety of climbing plants.

Alternate square or round stone columns in a classic Jekyll/Lutyens garden, designed and built before both materials and labour became so expensive.

Offset by the strong verticals of Italian cypress, large parasols give shade and echo the natural stone and rooflines of the nearby building.

The shingle roof of this boathouse prevents water collecting in the hull when the craft is not in use, and combines well with the rustic construction.

garden structures need not be entirely functional. This one defines the central space without dominating its surroundings.

Well suited to kitchen gardens, wands of hazel hoops can support sweet peas, runner beans or other climbing plants.

8

WATER

Moving water, whether fountains, cascades or waterfalls, can deliver the most magical of sounds. Fountains and pools need careful siting, as the noise of running water near the house is not always welcome.

Previous page Water can be a magical component in any garden. It should be placed carefully to maximize its reflective qualities, acting as a mirror and linking earth and sky. On a hot day the sound of water is cooling, and also detracts from less pleasant sounds such as traffic noise.

Water is a life force, a primal element, to which people are magnetically drawn. Water can act as a mirror, creating a link between the earth and the sky by reflecting clouds, tree canopies and garden features; it can transmit light; cool the air when present as an airborne spray; change colour as it takes in air; produce strong vertical displays; and deliver the most soothing and relaxing of sounds. Water can also be a transforming and tantalizing but expensive addition to your garden. In nature, it exists on the ground as seas, lakes and natural pools. Streams, cascades and waterfalls are a result of gravity and topography. Whilst mostly fluid, it can also exist as solid ice or as airborne water vapour. As a recreational focus, it can be used for paddling, swimming and fishing. However, if you are going to include water, then it needs to be thought about at the outset, before other landscaping work is undertaken, so that essential pipework or earth-shifting will cause the minimum of disruption to the rest of the garden.

Historically, water was included in gardens to grow plants, and for agriculture and sanitation. As aesthetics became more important, practicalities were often combined with a desire to enhance an overall composition: irrigation channels became rills and canals, baths and washing ponds doubled up as reflective formal pools. The Islamic and Moorish gardens were the first to show great skill in the use of water, but generally incorporating water for decorative purposes was rare in all but the finest houses until the Italian Renaissance. In Europe, at least, water features remained largely as still pools. The use of water in Chinese and Japanese gardens has always been more symbolic and spiritual. Comparing the use of water in the strict, formulaic and geometric European gardens of the seventeenth century with Japanese gardens of the same era would reveal how timeless the treatment in the oriental version is and how relevant it still remains today.

Climate plays an important role in deciding which type of water feature is most appropriate. Areas, or gardens characterized by much hard landscape, might benefit from cooling displays. In areas where there are cold winters and freezing conditions, shallow water is best and could even be used for winter sports such as skating. Parts of the world that do not experience climatic extremes – where water and light do not properly create the excitement that they arouse in hot countries – might be best suited to more natural uses of water, including developing wildlife habitats.

Formal pools cool the air and reflect light around gardens and more intimate spaces, especially if covered with glazed ceramic tiles. The choice of tile colour can define the character of the space.

Key design questions
All water features

➤ Is the climate and location suitable for a pond, pool or other water feature?

➤ What type of design is suggested by the immediate and wider context?

➤ What is the minimum depth of water required?

➤ What happens to excavated material?

➤ How will water be contained? What will happen if pipes, wires, etc. need to pass through the waterproof layer?

➤ Where will the water come from, especially for replenishment?

➤ How will the water level in the feature be controlled?

➤ How will the water quality be maintained? What equipment is needed?

➤ How will safety be guaranteed, especially if children are to interact?

➤ Will noise or reflections may affect neighbours?

➤ What maintenance operations will be required and how frequently?

➤ Could the addition of a change in level enhance the effect?

➤ Could moving water improve appearance? What pumps, pipes and electrical connections would be needed?

➤ Could lighting extend the effect?

Shallow rills carry water from one level to another, a copper 'lip' being used for the overflow. For a natural effect, allow moisture-loving plants to overhang the water.

Key design questions
Formal features

▸ Will the shape and size of the pool merge with its surroundings.

▸ What waterproofing should be used?

▸ What will the pool base and sides look like when seen through the water?

▸ How could appearance be improved?

▸ Should a fence be considered to limit access to children?

Water becomes most significant in garden design when it is exploited for its visual qualities. As with most aspects of garden design, the landscape or garden context will be important to its overall success. Waterfalls and cascades will always look odd in a flat landscape. Lakes or informal ponds tend to occur naturally at low points or depressions and will rarely look effective when perched half way up a slope or at the top of a hill. In a rural situation precedents will often come from nature, where clues can be taken from natural streams and riverbanks. Coastal areas might suggest beaches, upland areas, wetlands or bogs. One frequently overlooked aspect is what should be done with excavated material. The process of digging a pond will generate volumes of material to be incorporated into the garden as mounds or other features. Taking the material off site is expensive and may not be practical.

Towns or built-up areas will usually demand a stronger, architectural response which leads to quite a formal design. However, placing a formal pool with stronger geometrical lines within a country or informal setting can also produce a dramatic effect, especially if combined with high-quality planting. Adding water as a point of interest can enhance an overall design theme or style. Generally, simplicity is preferable to unnecessary complexity. Views from inside buildings should be considered, especially at night when the interplay of water and light can produce an animated outdoor feature. Pools that are located close to buildings can also have the added benefit of reflecting light into nearby rooms.

For the best effect, position your water in an open, sunny space. Pools and ponds situated under trees will collect fallen leaves, which, as they decompose, will release toxic gases that might be harmful to wildlife. In shady places, small pools tend to look like puddles.

You need to ask the question, who is the water feature for? Wildlife obviously will have very different requirements to people. Ducks or domestic wildfowl might benefit from the protection of an island refuge. Fish will need deeper water and a healthy oxygenating environment. Marginal, emergent or submergent aquatic plants will require different depths of water. Nesting birds and aquatic mammals may also need specific habitats to survive.

Safety will be paramount, especially where young children have access to pool or pond. A child can drown in just 25mm(1in) of water. Steep-sided ponds and deeper pools may trap a falling child, so a means of escape must also be provided. But the problem is best avoided in the first place by limiting access.

Formal pools

The proportions of the house windows govern the size of the pool, uniting interior and exterior. For safety, a stone edge acting as a low wall raises the level of the pool.

A formal pool is rather like a bathtub. Most have a means of filling, a means of emptying, and a system to prevent overflow.

Formal pools can be constructed from a wide range of materials including timber, brickwork, reinforced or poured concrete, fibreglass, steel and stone. Most are based on combinations of low retaining walls, steps and ramps, but with the additional constraint of waterproofing.

FORMAL POOLS

A still, reflective pool is best suited to a sunny location.

Two or more layers can increase drama and excitement, especially if water falls between levels.

Singular stones or artefacts can be used as a basis for a water feature.

Shallow, non-reflective pools must have attractive internal surfaces, often made from mosaic or decorative ceramic and stone tiles. Reflective surfaces need a dark background and a shallow viewing angle, which can be achieved with pigments, paint, dark liners or grey/black stones such as slate, basalt or granite.

The overall shape should fit with surrounding patterns and geometry. Water level can be almost flush with the surface or set below an overhanging edge, which will cast a shadow, hiding any awkward detail of what occurs when it meets the high water level.

Small pools, up to 8mx5m(approximately 26x16ft) can be relatively easily constructed using mass *in situ* concrete, 150mm(6in) thick or concrete blocks.

Informal ponds

In many parts of the world, the simple act of digging a hole is all that is needed to create a pond. Water tends to gather at low points and can sit just below the surface if there is a high water table. If the soil or geology are suitable, then the water will be held in place. Naturally fed lakes, ponds and streams will always require the least maintenance and will sit most effectively into the landscape. Decisions will, however, need to be made about the overall shape, bank profile, water source and inlet, outfall and overflow, methods of waterproofing and means of replenishment. 'Natural' ponds located within a highly urban area or a small domestic garden will generally look unnatural, although even the smallest body of water might provide a valuable habitat for urban wildlife.

Ponds created for wildlife need to be carefully planned. If fish are intended, then the pond should be at

Informal pools make a positive ecological addition to gardens but can be almost unnoticeable where water plants and algae meet. Ponds can be dangerous unless fenced off and carefully managed.

Stream-hugging contours

Lake/pond in natural depression

Outfall/overflow

Variety of edge treatments

Try to take a lead from natural streams and ponds when incorporating water artificially into gardens.

least 600mm(2ft) deep, even deeper if the water is likely to freeze in winter. The pond should also have a wide surface area to absorb oxygen; and be profiled to allow suitable plant species to be introduced and to thrive. Water quality will be critical and it may be worth consulting a specialist to advise upon maintaining the quality of natural water, or changing the properties of treated water. Wildlife and pesticides do not mix, so any garden maintenance that involves highly toxic herbicides should be kept well clear of water in order to prevent the possibility of polluting groundwater.

For a natural effect, edge profiles for pools should be planted, leaving a few areas accessible to allow a close-up view of water life, such as dragon flies or fish and to vary views.

Try to mimic local geological conditions. In rocky areas, water can be made to fall or cascade over artificial rock formations and still look effective. Imported rocks in lowland or flat areas can look like a garden centre display and be totally out of character with the area. Try to mimic natural geological strata, which often slope and tend to be characterized by bedding layers.

It will be important to understand the existing levels and gradients of the garden. On a sloping site, a large pond or small lake, for instance, would require some deep excavations into the slope and a large dam to contain the water. It might be better

Key design questions
Informal ponds and lakes

➤ If a naturalistic pond or lake is required, will the topography allow the water to appear natural?

➤ Are the bank profiles safe and suitable for healthy plant growth?

➤ Are the edge treatments stable and sufficient to prevent erosion?

to use a series of smaller water bodies separated by weirs, waterfalls or cascades. Perhaps a simple stream might be best of all. In addition to understanding existing ground levels, the impact of excavations and the resulting surplus material should be planned for. A pond 1m(3ft3in) deep will produce a mound over 1m(3ft3in) high. In flatter areas this might provide an occasion for an interesting sculptural feature; and in an undulating landscape, this material could be easily spread and hidden. The impact of disposing of excavated material might affect surrounding surfaces and vegetation.

The bank profile should be designed with access, safety and habitat in mind. Do not create slopes steeper than 1:3 and preferably 1:5. Marginal aquatics will be affected by very subtle changes in water level, the height of which can be controlled by an outfall and weir. Unless it is being constantly replenished, evaporation will

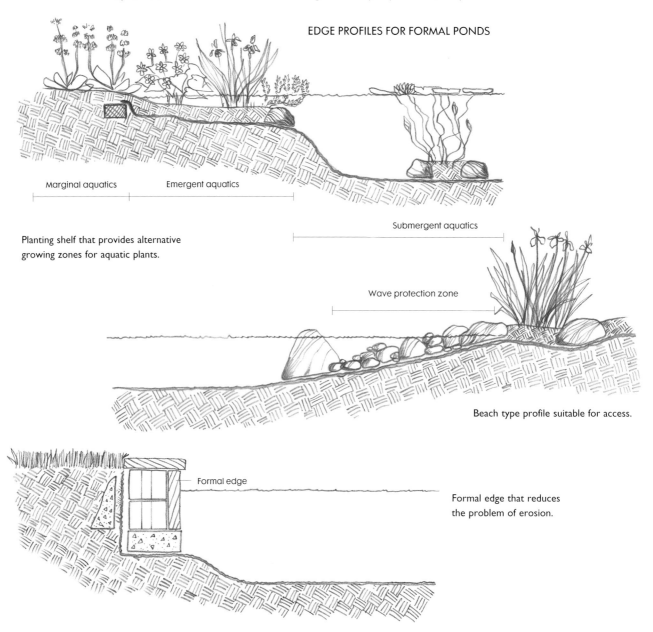

EDGE PROFILES FOR FORMAL PONDS

Marginal aquatics   Emergent aquatics

Submergent aquatics

Planting shelf that provides alternative growing zones for aquatic plants.

Wave protection zone

Beach type profile suitable for access.

Formal edge

Formal edge that reduces the problem of erosion.

cause the level to drop. If it fluctuates, then plant species that are adapted to these conditions should be selected. A planting shelf 200mm (8in) below water level will provide an alternative growing zone to which many emergent species are adapted; floating and submergent aquatics can be located in deeper water. Wildfowl and small mammals may have particular requirements for access. Waterproofing systems, especially liners, will be affected by burrowing animals and invasive plants such as bamboo.

Larger lakes and ponds may benefit from the creation of one or more islands. These can provide a valuable safe habitat, as well as interesting design occasions, such as bridges, a small retreat building or an area for displaying sculpture.

Unlike formal pools, which tend to have hard edges, larger informal water bodies will be subject to erosion from wind and wave action, as well as physical wear at the edges from the footsteps of people and animals, which can wash away soil and reveal unattractive waterproofing membranes. The design of the edge, grassed, planted or reinforced with harder, heavier material, will need to take erosion into account.

Timber has a special affinity with water and allows close access to the edge.

Dams, weirs, waterfalls and cascades

Changes of level between bodies of water provide some of the most exciting design opportunities. Water can fall freely away from vertical surfaces; bounce over rocky outcrops or slip over the face of the wall. The height of weirs and dams will control the level of the contained water, so levels can be manipulated very accurately.

Nature enhanced. In areas where puddle clay prevails, stone or timber 'falls' can be constructed to emphasize the meandering path of the water. As in nature, water should always be seen to occur at the lowest level of ground.

Natural stone mimics a rocky outcrop

Formal rill and weir

Constructed weir of timber and tin

Proportions of height to width need to be carefully planned for cascades. The weirs need to be carefully constructed so that water does not flood round the perimeter edges and spoil the effect. A pump will be needed to control the flow of water.

Dams and weirs must be waterproof in order to contain water. They must also be strong or heavy enough to stay in place. Traditionally, a dam would have been made from clay or compacted earth, covered with a waterproofing material. The front face would normally have been planted or grassed, and the shape designed to work with the surrounding topography. But modern building techniques, and the problems of moving earth around with restricted access, have meant that today dams in gardens are often made from concrete or blockwork with turf pushed up against them, rather

Opposite **The scale of this pool and water cascade make a bold statement. Uplighters enliven the evening scene, creating nocturnal reflections on the flat surface.**

Adding moving water to gardens which are used in the evening can create playful displays of light as well as soothing sounds.

like a retaining wall. Weirs are different: because the water in a weir flows over the surface, it can wash away the soil or subsoil itself; so, traditionally, heavy stones were laid down to resist erosion. Some stones may have been mortared together in a more controlled fashion. Using natural stone is still one of the best methods of changing levels within a natural stream, although the detailing will depend on the overall theme, style

WATER EFFECTS

Chute

Wall mounted head

Quiet stream

Turbulent stream

or context of the water channel. If a waterproof liner is being used, then this will need to be carefully integrated into, or under, the weir.

When designing a waterfall an important consideration will be how the water falls from one level to another. A full sheet of water falling consistently over an accurate horizontal edge will produce a highly controlled curtain of water, the intensity of which will be determined by the depth (i.e. volume) of water at the edge. Deliberate interruptions in the horizontal rim or edge of the upper water body will produce a broken sheet, and placing projections from the wall behind the curtain will cause the water to bounce and catch air and light.

Water can be directed away from a wall or vertical surface along a chute or from a spout. However, If channelled through a narrow aperture, water tends to stick to itself so that a flat sheet becomes more triangular as it meets the ground.

If there is insufficient water flowing over the edge, water tends to double back on itself and cling to the underside of the projected chute, producing an unsatisfactory effect. A small drip groove located on the underside of the overhanging edge will help prevent this. Most of these effects are produced by designing an upper water body which is allowed to flow across one or more edges, rather like an overflowing bowl. The smoothness of the edge is important. If it is made from a number of smaller units or from metal sheets that have been welded together, then it will be critical that the joints be absolutely flush to prevent the water surface breaking as it flows over the edge.

Waterfalls and water chutes create noise – one of the best reasons for placing them in a garden. Sound effects will be influenced by the height from which the water falls, its force and volume, the properties of the material on to which it falls and, if falling into open water, the depth of the water body below. By varying these features, noise can be manipulated to form a variety of different sounds – plops, splashes, slaps, burbles, and whooshes. Both high notes and low notes can also be achieved. But bear in mind how your beautiful sound might affect less impressed neighbours, especially at night.

A method of controlling pumped water as it flows over equally spaced falls, a rill can can emphasize axis and geometry and also provide a pleasant sound. The depth of water is usually fairly shallow.

WATERFALLS

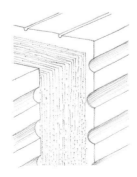

Aerated stream

Smooth stream

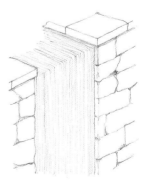

Full sheet

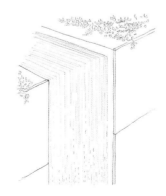

Broken sheet

Top over bottom – smooth floor

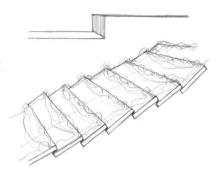

Bottom over top – aerated

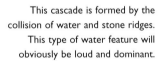

This cascade is formed by the collision of water and stone ridges. This type of water feature will obviously be loud and dominant.

Interrupting the flow of water as it moves across an inclined plane produces cascades. The effect is rather like water running over the tiles of a roof. If the tiles are placed with the top tile over the one below, then the water will flow freely over the surface. If however, the lower tile is placed on top of the one above it, then the water will hit the top edge of the lower tile as it flows down the slope. As it does so, it will break up, become aerated and turn white. The frequency of these interruptions, or how close they are placed together, will affect the intensity of the cascade. The construction of cascades is similar to that of ramps contained by retaining walls.

Fountains

Fan

Fountains can add energy and drama to garden design compositions. The ability of water to catch sunlight can produce illuminated columns of light, which will draw the eye or people towards it. If water is projected up into the air, it will free fall back to the ground, breaking up into tiny water droplets which will catch the light in different ways, depending upon their size, and produce showers and rainbows.

Some of the most dramatic fountains throughout history have been fed from a natural water source which relies on harnessing natural streams or significant volumes of water, located above the fountains so that they can be gravity fed. This situation is rare and, nowadays, most fountains are fed by pumped water. The inclusion of artificial pumps has many advantages. They allow the control of water patterns, height, volume of flow and timed effects, including arches and jumping jets. Furthermore, the wide variety of fountain nozzles means that many different shapes are available, such as fans, mushrooms, jets, domes, tulips, dandelions, bubbles and cones. It is also possible to generate mist, which can be used to reduce visibility or even as a type of external air conditioning, not to mention more ethereal effects.

Mushroom

Fountains can be designed to mix water and air together. This produces a more gentle flow which is white and frothy. Splash is reduced and the noise is less harsh.

Water can fall into a pool, in which case the height of the fountains should generally be no bigger than the radius of the base pool, although in windy areas water can be blown horizontally three of four times its height when it will not only create a potential hazard, but will also mean that water is lost from the pool. In this situation, it might be better to use smaller fountains associated with something more sculptural or ornamental. Many of the most famous historical fountains are combinations of water and art, most of which have become dramatic or symbolic focal points, away from the house or surrounding buildings or which may even have given a space its identity.

Dome

Below **Water droplets catch sunlight and can form form dancing displays.**

Water is very good at transmitting light, rather like a fibre-optic cable. If an intense source of light is positioned at the base of a fountain, then it will be transmitted through the water. At night, this can create dramatic effects and can be used to solve the common problem of how to improve an overlooked dark, dank courtyard.

A wall is a useful location for garden water, which might spout from a mask, ornament, or even a gargoyle. Metal pipes, chutes, tubes, found artifacts or specially commissioned pieces can be used as water sources. Water can be directed into bowls or basins where it can be collected, filtered and recirculated.

People, especially children, love to play and interact with water. Water can be fun, safe, cooling and sensuous. The addition of any water feature in a garden, however, needs careful consideration.

Single column

Aerated mass

Jumping jets

Multiple jets

PRACTICALITIES

Methods of waterproofing

The construction of structures designed to contain and channel water is based largely upon the principles of construction described throughout this book, but with the important difference that the containing surfaces must be waterproof. The selection of a method of waterproofing will be determined by the accuracy required to achieve a final shape, its overall appearance, cost and size. Generally, informal ponds and lakes are treated differently to constructed and more formal pools, especially those that involve complicated changes in level. Bodies of water constructed or created below surrounding ground level will inevitably differ fundamentally from those above ground level.

Below ground structures, such as lakes and ponds, may require no waterproofing at all. If they are naturally fed and if the soil and underlying geology is impermeable, then water that is collected will tend to remain in place, being naturally topped up as it outfalls or evaporates. In most gardens, however, conditions will not be suitable and it will be necessary to use an artificial means of waterproofing. Historically, and in more rural areas,

where clay is plentiful, landscape designers like Capability Brown would use a 300mm(1ft)-layer of material that would be puddled, or trampled, to remove the air. As long as this puddled clay stays permanently wet, then it will remain waterproof and can last for centuries. It is also the most environmentally sensitive method, but if it is allowed to dry out, may leak and then require regular maintenance. More commonly, in garden situations, artificial liners are used. Technology is changing all the time, but the two most common materials are butyl rubber and PVC. Both are suited to free-form shapes and usually come with a 25-year guarantee. Sheets can be box welded or glued together, although this is a specialist operation. Smaller ponds can be made from a single sheet without the need for joints. Specialist advice will be needed if there is a naturally high water table, as the pressure of water underneath a liner can cause it to blow up into an enormous bubble; a pump may be needed below the liner to alleviate the problem. Artificial liners are prone to puncturing and most of the care and effort in design and construction is associated with the prevention of leaks. If the liner were to lose its waterproofing integrity, it would be almost impossible to locate the source of the problem, so all forms of liner must be sandwiched between layers of puncture-resistant material, such as a geotextile felt membrane, and covered with at least 25mm(1in) of

WATERPROOFING A POND OR LAKE USING AN ARTIFICIAL LINER

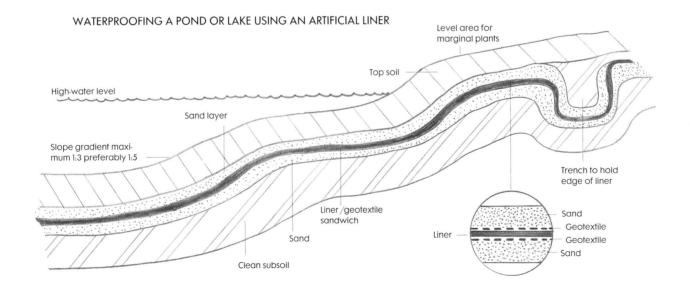

clean sand, both above and below the liner. Most materials are susceptible to the damaging effects of ultraviolet light, and it is important to make sure that the whole liner is fully covered.

The edges of larger, artificially lined water bodies, such as ponds or lakes, need to be protected against wave action. Most often this can be achieved through the addition of heavy stones or pebbles to create a beach type effect sometimes known as rip rap. Without this, soil would be washed away unless it were bound together by the roots of plants, or an artificial mesh. Because liners are slippery, soil will slide off slopes steeper than 1:3. The edges of the liner must be buried in a trench or held in place by heavy stones or construction.

Poured concrete is easily cast or trowelled into different shapes, is reasonably economic and durable. Even complex or undulating shapes can be achieved by applying sprayed concrete (or 'Gunite') to steel reinforcement. Colour can be mixed into the cement matrix so that it becomes integral and therefore long-lasting. Painted and applied finishes are less durable, but afford a much wider range of colours. Waterproofing

agents will need to be added to the concrete mix, and the overall hand-finish must be watertight. Large areas of poured concrete will need expansion joints (in much the same way as do cast concrete paving slabs); these joints will need to be carefully detailed so that they are waterproof, usually through the inclusion of water-stop bars, cast into the slab. Poured concrete is also suitable for above ground structures, which are designed and built in much the same way as retaining walls, the main difference being that water, rather than earth, will be supported. Reinforcement should be included, and the junction between the floor slab and vertical wall given careful attention. New concrete will leak lime, which harms plant and animal life. New ponds should therefore be filled, cleaned and emptied at least three times before any plants or wildlife are introduced.

The major advantage of using concrete for pools above ground is that the internal and external surfaces can be covered with a decorative facing, such as tiles or mosaic, which should be bonded with a cement-based adhesive and waterproof grout. For smaller pools, and in situations where varying levels and rectilinear shapes are required, it may be easier and more cost-effective to use

It is difficult to create an accurate container for a flat sheet of water using heavy building materials. Here a thin metal strip is set into the top of the wall.

EDGE TREATMENTS SUITABLE FOR FORMAL POOLS

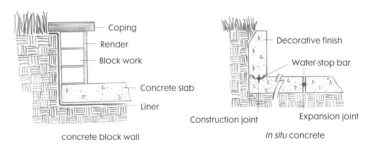

concrete block wall

In situ concrete

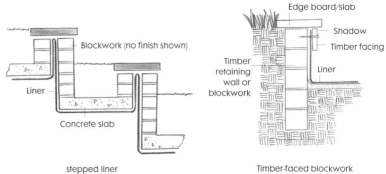

stepped liner

Timber-faced blockwork

A clean stone edge reflected in the pool makes a crisp conjunction between vegetation and water.

totally waterproof container. It is messy and expensive and best left to a specialist. Great control over water levels, waterfalls, rills and cascades can be achieved by constructing fibreglass, metal or plastic containers to accurate dimensions based on detailed design drawings. Trays, boxes, chutes, overflows and other crisp shapes can be fabricated from sheet material so long as the joints are fully waterproof. All can be drilled to receive pipes and other fittings, such as simple effective connectors, and domestic plumbing fittings can be used to ensure watertight joints. Many off-the-peg pools are available which are quick and easy to install.

Because most waterproofing layers will need to be breached or perforated in order to allow pipes, electrical

concrete blocks. The use of smaller units allows more control over the detailing of shapes and sizes, but the joints between them can leak over time. Blockwork should be rendered with 1:6 cement: sand mix with an added waterproofing agent, and pigment if required. Brushing a liquid resin layer on to the finished surface will provide further protection.

Stone and brick are comparatively waterproof, but the joints between them are not. It is normal to build masonry walls on to and inside a liner so that effectively the walls remain fully saturated, the waterproofing being ultimately achieved by the liner. Careful detailing is needed to ensure a proper bond between the masonry and the liner. All stone and brick should be carefully selected or specified so that it is fully frost-resistant. Wooden pools are inexpensive and simple to construct. They can be designed in the same way as timber retaining walls, but must be waterproofed either on the inside, between the timber and the water, or behind the timber which will become permanently saturated. Treated timber may ooze toxic compounds and if the timber is directly in contact with the water, it would be better to use untreated hardwood. When selecting edge materials, remember that some are suited to being in water, whilst others are more suited to being next to water.

Specialist suppliers and contractors offer other methods of waterproofing. The most flexible and problem free system uses fibreglass, which is built up in layers into a

Colourful tiles and mosaics can be easily seen through shallow water but are best suited to hot, sunny areas.

connections, lights and overflows to pass through the layers, it will be critically important to plan ahead. Most commercially available pumping systems are supplied with special sealing gaskets and valves, but very careful thought must be given to this aspect of the design before you begin.

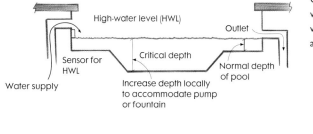

Overflows and outlets will control the high-water level. Sensors allow automatic replenishment.

Depth of water

For decorative purposes water in any feature need only be a few millimetres (less than an inch) deep, especially if it is flowing over attractive natural stone or metal. Generally, water bodies seldom need to be more than 700mm(2ft3in) deep, and 400mm(1ft3in) is often sufficient. If greater depth is required for a particular reason, such as to hide a fountain nozzle, as a habitat for submergent aquatic planting or for play, then the extra depth should normally be achieved locally rather than across the whole area

In cold climates water must be sufficiently deep to avoid freezing, especially if fish are resident. Shallow ponds should normally be drained in winter or heated to avoid risk of frost.

Open bodies of water with little circulation will need to be deeper, often 1m(3ft3in) or so. If ponds and lakes are too shallow, they will heat up. As warm water contains less oxygen it may kill any fish, while the water tends to stagnate much more rapidly.

Loss of water from evaporation will vary greatly throughout the climatic regions. In the UK evaporation is minimal, but in hotter climates can be very significant. Leakage is more of an issue, and accounts for most rapid drainage problems. One-way valves should also be included to prevent the whole system from draining itself.

Water quality and water flow

If water is being used for aesthetic effects, then it is best to obtain it from a treated domestic supply. Any water feature connected to a main's supply will need to have domestic shut-off valves and safety cut-outs to avoid flooding if the replenishment systems fail. Automatic top-up tanks or cisterns can detect water level and introduce more water should the level drop significantly. Sensors can also be added to detect low temperature (i.e. freezing conditions), high winds and no-flow blockages, automatically switching off pumps and other systems.

In natural ponds, and certainly where wildlife is introduced or encouraged, untreated water would be preferable. A proper biological balance of nutrients, and in particular oxygen, should be established before any plants or animals are introduced. The addition of taller plants to photosynthesize and release oxygen will help fish, and will also starve lower plants of carbon dioxide, helping to keep the water healthy.

Water pressure and flow rates will only be important if water is pumped or moved around. The pressure of water will come from gravity (i.e. how high the source is above the outlet) or the size of the pump. It is best to consult a specialist and to describe the effect you would like. In general, it is usually best to use a pump which is slightly more powerful than you need. In open water

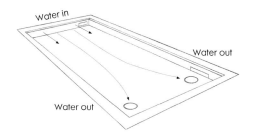

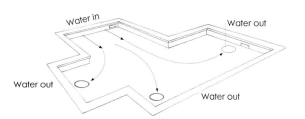

In order to avoid areas of formal pools and ponds becoming stagnant, locate water outlet or pumps to encourage circulation throughout.

areas and in oblong formal pools, water can become stagnant at the ends and in corners. Re-circulation systems should draw water from the extremities and introduce fresh or filtered water at the opposite end so that it is kept moving.

Pumps, plumbing and connections

Selecting the correct pump requires advice from an expert. Make sure you know exactly what you are trying to achieve. Submersible or underwater pumps tend to last longer and are more efficient, but do present problems if they need maintaining. There are also potential concerns about electrical safety. External (or remote) pumps are easy to access in case of break down, but can be noisy and are less durable. Amateurs can install low voltage systems, but a qualified electrician must install main's voltage. It is essential to incorporate an RCD (Residual Current Device) or circuit breaker to protect people and electrical circuits should a problem arise. All underground electrical cabling should be armoured. Ideally, the pumps, timers, light sensors, display effects and other electrical devices should be remotely controlled from inside the house.

Water used for decorative purposes, which needs to be kept clean, must be filtered. Combinations of sand filters and ultraviolet filters, introduced into re-circulation systems, will keep the water clean, but will require regular maintenance. Sand filters, for example, will

In a warm climate it is possible for pools to be effective in cool, shady places, whereas in cooler climates they can become dark and dank.

SCHEMATIC REPRESENTATION OF WATER CIRCULATION AND ELECTRICAL COMPONENTS

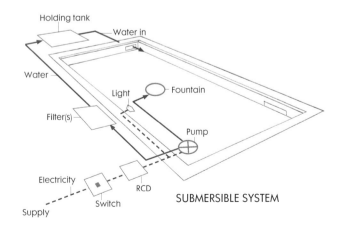

Holding tank
Water in
Water
Light — Fountain
Filter(s)
Pump
Electricity
RCD
SUBMERSIBLE SYSTEM
Switch
Supply

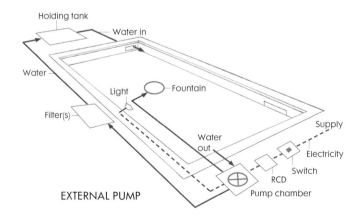

Holding tank
Water in
Water
Light — Fountain
Filter(s)
Supply
Water out
Electricity
Switch
RCD
EXTERNAL PUMP
Pump chamber

need to have their flow reversed to clean them regularly. Chemicals can be added to keep water clear, but these are generally toxic and smelly. Pumps always need to be kept clear of algae and debris.

When working with water outside, it is advisable to employ a qualified plumber or water specialist. Problematic connections can develop into expensive leaks that waste water. A good plumber will produce elegant pipe work with the minimum of material, joints and fixings, whereas an amateur could end up with something resembling the boiler room of an ocean liner.

Underground pipe work should be durable, and resistant to damage by vermin and garden tools. Most crucially, the size of the pipes and the flow within them will determine the volume of water and therefore the ultimate effect.

Although the detail in this chapter may sound daunting, the inclusion of water is a magical asset in any garden; it is also often the most complex. By understanding the complexities, you should be able to have a sensible and productive discussion with an experienced contractor – the first step in realizing your vision.

Fountains and cascades in many historical gardens, seen here at Villa d'Este, were based upon gravity-fed sytems, now comparatively easy to acheive on a domestic scale with new technology.

Single or multi-jet fountains can be installed to flow at varying frequencies. The sound of water should be tuned to the surrounding space.

Water lilies and other aquatic plants add interest to the surface of this small formal pool.

A large stone slab is all that is needed to bridge this gap in a garden containing no artificial materials.

A wall-mounted mask provides a steady flow of water, with a cascade shown off by the mossy backdrop.

Still or slow-moving water is calming and relective, and works well with uncluttered grassy banks.

A metal box contains a flat mirror-like sheet of water, making surrounding vertical elements appear taller and more dramatic.

The smallest waterfall produces a relaxing sound that draws attention and detracts from surrounding noise.

Concentric circles and water, such as these ripples, are always calming. Here they are produced from thin metal set into a shalow pool.

Any container which holds water can be incorporated into a garden where it will provide an alternative area for plants and wildlife.

Shady areas can be home to good ponds too, but will need regular maintenance as they collect a lot of leaves and encourage weed and algae.

Water dripping into the copper bowl produces gentle ripples. A possible place for meditation.

Deeply planted edges and a summerhouse enhance the tranquil nature of this small pond.

These glowing columns are formed by beams of sunlight hitting water droplets produced by small misting devices.

Multiple jets are a magnet to children. They are often computer controlled and produce a dramatic display, but may be prohibitively expensive.

Colour and materials contrast to form this simple but classic and much-used piece of design.

Still, reflective water is punctuated by ground glass stepping stones which, because of cleverly designed supports, appear to float over the surface.

The long-standing chute or spout-and-bowl idea has been carefully sculpted into an organic form which combines well with arching grasses and ferns.

Stone steps, here, make a stream bed with water cascading over. It would be tempting to try to ascend without getting your feet wet.

MATERIALS

This section covers most of the materials in current use. Modern building materials are developing rapidly and it may may be worth looking at current magazines, visiting a builders merchant or even attending a local trade show to seek out the latest innovative or alternative materials.

Aggregate

The term aggregate refers to a useful range of naturally occurring sands and gravels, crushed stone, manufactured products, including furnace slag and ash, vermiculite and recycled crushed building materials, such as crushed concrete and brick. They are used loose and untreated as paving and surfaces for roads, to protect slopes, as a mulch and as a base for paving units. These sands and aggregates are the major component of concrete and mortar.

Selection criteria will be based upon strength, durability (hardness and life expectancy), resistance to weathering and freezing without decomposing, solubility and resistance to chemical reactions. Where they will remain visible, appearance will also be important. Sands and aggregates should be clean and free from clay and silt particles, salts and organic matter.

The colour range of the aggregate comes from the origin of the naturally occurring sand, gravel or stone – for instance, granite produces a black, grey, green, or pink aggregate; sandstone results in brown, red, or terracotta shades; slate chips in grey, and quartzite in white, pink, or golden tones.

Aggregate is specified by defining a range of particle sizes. Typically small sizes are 2–6mm($\frac{1}{20}$–$\frac{1}{4}$in); medium sizes 6–10mm

($\frac{1}{4}$–$\frac{1}{2}$in); large sizes 10–20mm($\frac{1}{2}$–$\frac{3}{4}$in) and 20mm($\frac{3}{4}$in) plus. Paths normally require two layers with larger sized aggregate being used to provide structural strength below, and smaller (and decorative) aggregates being used at the surface. Where surfaces need to lock together, it is best to use a range of sizes, including specifying crushed stone '10mm($\frac{1}{2}$in) to dust', meaning everything that passes through a 10mm($\frac{1}{2}$in) sieve.

Concrete

Concrete is a mixture of cement, sand, aggregate and water. When water is added, a chemical reaction occurs, which causes hardening. Full strength is achieved after about 28 days, as moisture remains available.

There are typically five or six types of cement available, suitable for different situations and applications; numerous sands from different origins, of different colour and particle size; a wide range of aggregates, also of varying colour and strength characteristics. These can be combined in many different ways to make the mixture strong, attractive, easily poured, sprayed, finished once hard, able to mimic natural stone, durable and lightweight, etc. It is clearly a complex business and, in all but the most basic of uses, for example, as foundations for walls and pavements, specialist advice is needed.

Most of the strength comes from the aggregate, and so stronger stone (granite, basalt) will make a stronger mix than soft aggregate such as limestone. Appearance comes from the colour of the cement (usually light grey and resembling Portland stone – hence the name Portland cement); from sand (ranging from silver white to

earthy reds and browns); from aggregate (see above) especially when revealed as exposed aggregate finish, tooled and polished finishes; and from added pigments. White Portland cements are available and are best for light-coloured concrete or where pigments are added.

Types of cement and basic concrete mixes are shown opposite. Concrete must be mixed by a skilled person to ensure that the consisitency and strength are correct.

Cement
Ordinary Portland Cement (OPC) Used for most brickwork and blockwork above ground.
Sulphate Resisting Cement (SRC) Used below ground and in wet/marine conditions; also used if bricks have higher than normal levels of soluble salt.
White Portland Cement (WPC) Used for restoration work or for careful colour matching of light coloured mortars and concretes. Useful for rendering because of its light colour, as it has some water resistance. It is expensive.
Rapid Hardening Portland Cement (RHPC) Used where timing is crucial, such as retaining walls at low temperatures. It dries to working strength in 24 hours instead of 28 days for OPC.

Mortar mixes

Mortar is used to bond building units together; to compensate for surface irregularities in stone, brick and blocks; to allow for variation in the size of bricks when laying courses; and as a controlled bedding layer for thin paving units. It may also have a very significant effect on the overall appearance of the construction and is not merely a functional element.

Mixtures are based upon strength, workability and appearance. Options include:

Concrete mixes			
Mix	Former volumetric classification	Applications	Volumetric proportions (Cement:: damp sand: aggregate)
C7.5P (1500 psi)	1:3:6	Footings, foundations, oversite concrete, mass concrete	2:5:8
C20P (3000 psi)	1:2:4	*In situ* slabs, small retaining walls	3:5:9
C25P (4000 psi)	1:1:3	Reinforced concrete, mass concrete walls	3:4:7
C7.5P is a UK prescribed mix, 7.5 standing for the strength designation 7.5N/mm^2 (US PSI)			

- Cement, sand and water
- Cement, lime, sand and water
- Lime, sand and water
- Cement, lime, plasticizer and water

(Lime gives workability; and cement, frost-restisance.)

Mortar for brickwork and blockwork outdoors is normally a mix of OPC and sand in proportions between 1:3 and 1:6. Below ground or for heavy blockwork applications, 1:3 is better.

The colour of the sand will have the most dramatic effect on appearance. Use washed soft sand for bricklaying; rendering or sharper sand for render.

Lime, added to maintain some flexibility in the mortar, is useful when working with reclaimed materials. Lime is Important in restoration work or in old damp buildings, where cement may not be used at all. It is now largely replaced with plasticizers. Cement lime mortars are generally mixed in the proportions (cement:lime:sand) 1:1:6 for general purpose and 1:¼:4 for stronger mortar requirements. Cement mortar is the strongest, but should only be used with strong bricks.

Additives include plasticizers to provide more flexibility to the mortar to speed up work and provide some enhanced frost resistance. Proofers can improve protection against water damage. Colourants can be used to match or complement masonry materials. In large jobs this is best specified from a specialist mortar supplier to avoid problems with colour matching between different batches.

Selecting render

Cement-sand render is a type of mortar that is used on vertical surfaces as an aesthetic finish. It is not always better to use a stronger mix. The higher the proportion of cement, the greater the chance of cracking – especially in render.

Generally, use two layers of render with a mix of cement: lime: sand of 1:1:6. On stronger, less porous surfaces use a mix of 1:½:4½ or 1:¼:3 for the base layer with a 1:1:6 top coat.

Precast concrete slabs

These are available in a range of sizes based upon 150mm(6in)-increments with common dimensions being 300mm(12in), 450mm(1ft6in), 600mm(2ft), and 900mm(3ft). Most are 35–40mm(¼in) thick.

Brick

Traditionally the size of a loaf, the size of bricks has now evolved over centuries into a unit that is very similar worldwide. Most countries have their own standard sizes, either based upon imperial measurements, standardized metric units or traditional sizes passed down through generations. The unit size is small enough so that one person can work all day without getting tired, but large enough to allow the building work to progress speedily.

Nearly all bricks are made from clay or concrete. Clay bricks weather beautifully and look better with age. Concrete bricks nearly always look synthetic and look worse with age. Where possible, use clay bricks where they will be seen, and cheaper concrete bricks where they will be hidden. Colours of clay bricks depend upon the type of clay used (the colour of natural clay deposits varying according to region), the firing process and temperature. For instance, in the UK, Midland bricks are red, while London bricks are yellow. Engineering bricks have a uniform colour and are not very attractive. Mottled and brindle bricks (sometimes known as multi-coloured) have a variable appearance, making them useful for large expanses. Handmade clay bricks are slightly variable in size and shape and look crafted, giving a special quality to finished surfaces and structures. As the colour of bricks will be typical to a locality, attention should be paid to matching, or at least using, bricks that are sympathetic to their surroundings. Dark reds, reds, russets, oranges, ochres, browns, blues, yellows, buffs, terracottas and other earthy colours are available.

UK sizes		
British Standard metric sizes		
Brick (standard)	215 x 102.5 x 65mm	
Paving block	200 x 100 x 60mm	
	200 x 100 x 40mm	
Dense concrete blocks	440 x 215 x 215mm	
	(also available hollow)	
	440 x 215 x 102.5	
	440 x 215 x 90	
	440 x 215 x 140	
US sizes		
Brick (standard)	3⅝ x 2¼ x 8in	
Brick Modular	3⅝ x 2¼ x 7⅝in	
Engineer brick	3⅝ x 2¹³⁄₁₆ x 7⅝in	
Economy 8 brick	3⅝ x 3⅝ x 7⅝in	
Blocks	15⅝ x 3⅝ x 7⅝in	
	15⅝ x 7⅝ x 7⅝in	
	11⅝ x 7⅝ x 7⅝in	
	Other combinations of 15⅝,	
	11⅝, 7⅝, 3⅝in	
NB Lightweight/thermal blocks have little load-bearing capacity and are not suitable for landscape use.		

Bricks used outdoors must be frost-resistant or protected from penetrating water by copings and damp-proofing layers.

Standard brick sizes are worked out to include the thickness of a mortar joint. Brick and joint dimensions co-ordinate so that multiples work together in a variety of ways to create bonding patterns without the need for cutting.

Choosing and specifying bricks

When choosing bricks, look for regularity in shape, size, colour and the rectangular face. A good brick should be well burnt and free of lime, cracks and stones. Colour is determined by the integral chemical composition of the raw clay and especially the amount of iron; red bricks contain about 5 per cent iron and

blue bricks 7–10 per cent. Although most bricks are made from clay, concrete bricks and calcium silicate bricks are also available, but much less attractive. You must specify size (see table on left), colour, surface finish/texture and any special shapes. Ideally specify by manufacturer and product code. Choose also whether you want frost-resistant (F) or moderately frost-resistant (M) bricks. Also you must decide on soluble salt content, which is either normal (N) or low (L). All bricks will be classified by both frost-resistance and soluble salt content. For example, a brick may be FN (frost-resistant, normal soluble salt content), ML (moderately frost-resistant, low soluble salt), etc.

Bricks with normal soluble salt levels may require Sulphate Resisting Portland Cement (SRPC). Moderately frost-resistant bricks will require protection from moisture penetration – especially at the tops of walls

Natural Stone

Crushed stone used as aggregate is discussed above. When used as masonry units in paving, as veneer, as tiles, as ornament or monument, the characteristics of the stone become relevant and important.

Sandstones are sedimentary rocks comprising fine sand and aggregate particles that are naturally cemented together. Sandstones can be sawn and tooled and are especially suited to paving due to their slip resistance. They are commonly used in walling as finely cut ashlar, as dressed stone or in rubble and drystone walls, where naturally present locally. Names in the UK refer to region of origin, for example, Yorkstone, Portland stone, Bath stone; in the USA names refer either to the region of origin or the colour of the stone, for example, Colorado rose, Wyoming pink, greystoke or scarlet.

Limestone is composed of calcium carbonate and magnesium carbonate naturally cemented by silica, iron oxide or lime carbonate, which gives the limestone from different regions a characteristic pattern and colour. Some limestones are highly figured, almost marble-like, and may contain fossils and other attractive components that can be exploited.

Limestone is chemically reactive and should not be used in areas subject to pollution or acids. Limestone is suitable for rubble walling and as a construction aggregate with the best stone being suitable as a veneer and in paving. Travertine is a type of highly figured limestone prized for its appearance and use as paving.

Marble is highly variable in appearance due to impurities and defects, as it is metamorphosed limestone. It is expensive, but beautiful and is used in the most prestigious gardens and buildings as paving, and in walling as a veneer or tile. Marble can be slippery as a surface. It is chemically reactive and will decay in high pollution.

Slate works well when used in tile or slab form for paving. It can be sawn or split along its bedding planes to produce a slightly undulating surface known as riven stone. Slate tends to be dark grey or greenish grey and is highly resistant to weathering and the effects of water, making it suitable for water features. Chipped slate can be used as a more informal path and as a mulch, but can get dirty and stick to the soles of shoes. It can also get slippery when wet.

Granite is a very strong and durable stone, that can be sawn or split for use in paving as slabs, cobbles and setts. It is also suitable for association with water, in walling and in monumental work. It can be cut into precise shapes, where it will hold its edge against wear. Colours include jet-black, greyish, pinkish and greenish, often with characteristic flecks and shiny micaceous facets.

Hoggin/fines

A word of unknown origin, hoggin is a mixture of sand and gravel or sifted gravel, used for paths as a base under a wearing course of gravel, or as a finished surface in its own right. Hoggin is a local term to the UK. In other parts of the world similar materials are referred to by other names; for example 'crusher fines', 'crusher run' and 'limestone fines' are all used in the USA. Provided there is a local source, it is a very economical path material, affording a solid and lasting random surface, well suited to rural areas.

As Hoggin is self-binding, it locks together to provide a firm surface without any additional cement, bituminous binder, or resin. A thin layer of gravel can be rolled onto well compacted hoggin to reduce the thickness of the loose material, avoiding the problem of too much loose gravel making it difficult to walk, as the gravel moves underfoot.

Reconstituted stone

Reconstituted stone is essentially a high quality concrete, which is uniform in appearance and available in a wide range of standard, usually traditional, shapes and as component parts of stylistic and historical masonry kits. It is made from finely graded stone dust and other fine aggregates and has a major advantage over pre-cast concrete in that cut and broken surfaces do not reveal ugly aggregates giving away the type of construction. It generally is designed to mimic sedimentary stones, especially sandstones and gritstones, but does not weather like natural stone and lacks the subtle beauty of grain, texture and minor imperfections that give natural stone its quality.

Timber

The terms hardwood and softwood do not refer to the constructional properties of the timber. Hardwood timber comes from broadleaved trees and softwood from coniferous species. However, in general terms hardwoods do tend to be denser than softwoods, making them more naturally durable and resistant to decay, but more difficult to work and obtain. Tropical hardwoods should not be used unless their provenance can be certified and guaranteed as coming from a sustainable resource.

Softwood timber can be prone to rot and decay at a much faster rate than hardwoods although some species, such as cedar and redwood, contain a lot of tannins and are naturally resistant. Timber can be treated with chemicals that prevent the material being fed upon by fungi or bacteria, which develops into rot. Treated timber can last for up to 50 years, but debate exists about the long-term environmental effects of these chemicals.

Specifying timber

Timber is specified by species and which part of the tree it comes from. Different species have different strength and durability characteristics, which have been fully tested worldwide with the results readily available from timber merchants and trade associations via the Internet. Cost, appearance, ease of working and availability will be important considerations and the final decision will often be a compromise between appearance, durability and cost. Where timber cannot be seen, cheaper and less attractive timber (for example that which has been downgraded for appearance) can be used so long as it meets strength requirements.

Good structural species include larch (treated), Douglas fir (treated), southern yellow pine, hemlock and fir. Good species for appearance with moderate strength include redwood and western red cedar. Cheaper species include Ponderosa pine and red pine both of which need treating.

Traditional hardwood species include oak, sweet chestnut and sycamore. Tropical hardwoods can be very durable, strong and attractive, but must be used responsibly.

Converted timber

Structural and decorative timber is 'converted' from the tree trunk by being cut into rectilinear boards, planks and other dimensioned timber. Different cuts produce a variety of appearances based on how the growth rings appear on the cut surface. This will also affect the stability of the board. The wood in the centre of the tree is inactive, usually very dense and decay-resistant, is known as heartwood. The outer region of the trunk, which is actively growing and transports water and nutrients, is known as sapwood. This tends to be less dense, may contain knots and other defects and is more prone to decay. In most garden structures, it is rare to use heartwood.

Timber cut radially from the outer edge towards the centre will produce boards with vertical grain that is resistant to cupping and warping. Trunks cut into parallel boards using parallel blades will produce boards with flat grain so that the end of the plank shows curved grain lines. This will tend to bow, warp, cup and twist.

Avoid timber that has splits and other crack-like defects (shakes and checks). Knots are not usually a problem, but may be unsightly, can fall out, and can ooze, causing staining to painted finishes if not treated. Wane is where the curved outer edge of the trunk appears on a board edge and can create problems matching edges in more detailed work, or where straight edges are needed. Do not buy warped boards. Look along the length of any timber and check for warps and twists.

Moisture content

It is important to use timber that is stable, and that will change shape and size only very minimally once incorporated into whatever garden structure is to be built. Timber is either air- or kiln-dried to allow moisture to drop to stable levels of less than 20 per cent, a level above which it is known as 'green'.

Sizing timber

Timber is measured as sawn dimensions, known as 'nominal size' – i.e. directly from the trunk. When it is planed to make it smooth it gets smaller so that a board 25x100mm will be that dimension in its sawn state, but may be 22x97mm when planed; possibly even smaller. As it dries out it may get smaller still. In the USA, a common 2x4m will be ($1\frac{1}{2}$in x $3\frac{1}{2}$in) after it has been surfaced on four sides, which is commonly referred to as S4S. Generally, take 4–5mm ($\frac{1}{2}$in) from sawn dimensions for planed timber dimensions.

Edge condition can also be specified. For decking, rounded or radiused edges are used to avoid splinters, but for more detailed work 'planed, square edge' (PSE timber), or 'planed all round' (PAR timber), is more common. Edge condition is less important in structural timber, which can be left with a cruder sawn finish, with the added advantage that the specified sizes will be more accurate.

Timber comes in standard dimensions and, where possible, it is best to design structures that minimize wastage or unnecessary joints. A deck 4.2m wide will use a standard length. A deck 4.3m would require another board, or a cut from a

longer length. In the USA wood comes in 2ft increments, so when designing, work towards 8, 10, 14 and 16ft lengths to save cutting.

Grading

Timber is graded at the sawmill for strength, defects, moisture content and certification. Some wood may be graded for appearance: with (knotty), or without knots (clear grade). Different species are graded in different ways.

Pressure treatment

All timber used outdoors should be resistant to weathering, either though natural tolerance, good design or chemical treatment.

Softwood timber is usually pressure-treated by using chemicals that prevent the decay and rot caused by fungi, bacteria and insects. It is possible to paint the chemicals onto the surface, but this is less effective. The mix of water-borne chemicals usually includes chromated copper arsenate (CCA), or involves replacing arsenic with boron as (CCB). Toxicity is locked into the timber once dry and should remain environmentally benign, although there is some debate on this. Avoid creosote, which is more toxic.

Boards

Timber, fibre and composite boards are useful materials with which to construct simple planters, panels for garden structures and fences and as bases for treehouses and sandpits. Thinner boards, especially plywood, are also useful for curved details, including path edging, planters and as formwork for poured concrete. The main board material for use outdoors is WBP (weather and boil proof) plywood (called Marine Ply in the USA), available in standard 2440x1220mm (8x4ft)- boards and 3, 6, 12 and 19mm($\frac{1}{8}$, $\frac{1}{4}$, $\frac{1}{2}$, $\frac{3}{4}$in) thick. Blockboard is very strong, but not especially attractive and in the USA has

largely been replaced with particleboard. Neither is the best product for outdoor use. Particleboard is available up to 25mm(1in) thick. MDF is not suitable for exterior use.

Metals

The ability to bend and shape metal into intricate and delicate patterns, combined with high strength to weight and design traditions makes metal a valuable material in gardens. Many people shy away from working with metal because of the specialist skill and equipment required to achieve high quality results. However, some careful forward planning and the involvement of a specialist can have rewarding results.

The most common types of metal used in gardens are ferrous metals (cast iron, wrought iron, carbon steels and stainless steel), aluminium and aluminium alloys, and copper or copper alloys (brass, bronze). Selecting the most appropriate metal will be based upon appearance, strength, tradition, cost, ability to work to the required shape and resistance to corrosion.

Grey cast iron was the structural metal used in the early nineteenth century. Containing more than 2 per cent carbon, it is easily cast in sand moulds when molten, but is brittle and therefore easily broken. It cannot be bent and is susceptible to corrosion. It is used mainly for garden furniture, tree grilles, gulley gratings and in garden restoration.

Ductile iron is stronger in tension, and more suitable for heavy-duty outdoor work. It can be poured and traditionally was used to make large and heavy components, such as pipes, gateposts, bollards and bespoke details. Both types of iron are easily moulded and more rust-resistant than untreated steel.

Wrought iron has a much lower carbon content which makes it more malleable and easier to weld and manufacture. It is hammered under heat to increase its tensile strength, and is suitable for bending and forging at low temperatures. Many forms are available based upon rods, bars, sheets and plates – which can be combined into fences, gates, trellis, railings, grilles and other shapes by skilled blacksmiths.

Carbon steel is produced by adding manganese, silicon and copper to iron. It is extremely strong and is easily joined and fixed. It is available as sheet material, structural components (beams and columns), reinforcement (rods and mesh), wire, chain link, mesh and other special shapes. Carbon steels must be protected against weathering.

Weathering steels, such as CorTen® steel, contain a small amount of copper and sometimes chromium. As they have an iron oxide coating, the rust does not fall off when in contact with air. They are strong, work well in sheet form – acting as retaining devices or planters – but they are also available in similar shapes to other forms of steel. They are expensive, but maintenance-free, the rusted form which weathers to a brownish-purple finish being popular in contemporary design. But it can stain surrounding surfaces and is not resistant to salt attack, so it must not be submerged in water or used in seaside locations, or buried.

Stainless steels have chromium added as well as some nickel and other minor metals. They are highly resistant to weathering, have high strength and a shiny long-lasting appearance, of particular use in coastal areas, as the salts will not rust it. It is also useful for structures where galvanizing or painting is difficult. They are initially very expensive but require almost no maintenance and useful for high- quality components, handrails, furniture and fixings. Welding is a specialist operation, best carried out in the factory.

Aluminium, the most widely used non-ferrous material, is lightweight, strong and corrosion-resistant except when used adjacent to cement, lime and concrete, when it can decay. It is naturally a silvery grey colour, but is vulnerable to lime staining caused by bird droppings. It can take a high polish, but is easily scratched; anodising gives it a harder surface. It is mainly used in fabricated form as angles, channels and bars and to hold glazing, or for lightweight fittings and items designed to be moved by hand.

Copper is easily worked, half the weight of lead, relatively non-toxic and can have a shiny finish or, when exposed to the weather, be allowed to oxidise to a greenish patina known as verdigris. Copper can be cast and welded, rolled or drawn. It is commonly used for plumbing components, for holding and carrying water in tanks and pipes, for flashing on water features, for damp-proof courses, for copings on brick walls, for planters, roofing, and ornamental elements, which can be commissioned. Very thin copper sheet or foil can be bent around simple timber posts.

Zinc is resistant to corrosion; it is used for roofing and as a coating in galvanizing, or as a substitute for copper sheeting.

Lead is best known for seventeenth-century cast figurines and cisterns; it is corrosion-resistant when exposed to air. It is also resistant to most acids and other building materials. Highly toxic, it should never be used near edible plants or where children play. Make sure that it is well maintained and that any leaching will not be harmful.

Alloys, such as brasses and bronzes, are used mainly in the form of sculpture and containers.

Protecting metal against corrosion

Different metals decay in different ways – usually known as corrosion. This is a chemical reaction that occurs when either two incompatible metals are in contact with each other or when a single metal is in contact with water, or both. Water will normally need to be present, although this can be in the form of air-borne moisture. If moisture cannot be controlled, then surfaces will need to be protected by painting, coating with a moisture-proof barrier (plastic, bitumen), avoiding incompatible metals, or by adding another metal that purposefully corrodes onto the surface and protects it, such as zinc coatings onto iron (galvanising). Damaged areas may need further protection.

Never have different materials touching without checking on their compatibility, and ideally make all parts from the same metal. All metals will stain, for example the verdigris from copper sheeting will stain concrete green; or metal fixed to oak timbers may rust because of the tannin. If in doubt, seek specialist advice.

Metal finishes

Some metals, such as stainless steel, brass, copper and self-oxidising (weathering) steel, do not need finishing. Others need protecting with certain galvanized coatings (e.g. bright zinc plate or BZP), selected for their appearance. Galvanizing involves the coating of the metal surface with molten or a dry powder of zinc; it will then weather more slowly, but will eventually break down. Lead, cadmium, tin and zinc can all be used to protect the surface and alter the appearance, although zinc is the most common for external use. Any coatings or protective layers are best applied after the metal has been formed and welded.

Colourful options include primers and paint (some that need no priming), enamels, and applied plastic coatings (dipped plastic or baked-on powder coating), which need very little attention. All are available in the whole colour spectrum although compatibility between finish and metal should be checked. Before applying the primer or paint, first remove oil and grease by wiping with a weak acid, then rinse in clean water. Prime with one coat of epoxy zinc phosphate primer, then two coats of finish; first a high build epoxy resin, then a final coat of enamel paint. Vitreous enamel is applied as molten glass to protect metal surfaces and the finishes are less prone to fading. All paint finishes require maintenance and will fade in ultra violet light.

Plastic, nylon, or PVC coating – suited to chain-link fences or similar – is applied by first treating the metal with an electrically-charged polyester dust, available in a limited colour range, and fixed by electrical attraction. To alter its appearance, metal can also be polished or sandblasted; treated chemically to produce various colours and textures; and heated or anodized (with an electric current).

Thermal fastening
Metal can be fixed with mechanical fixings (described below) or by welding, soldering and brazing. Welding joints involves heating the two pieces to be joined to melting point with or without a filler, then placing them together to create the bond. Brazing and soldering involve the introduction of another filler material that melts at a lower temperature than the pieces of metal to be joined.

Fixings

Many garden structures are fixed together with metal screws, bolts, nails, rivets and plate fixings that are available in numerous shapes, sizes, finishes and types of metal, which can be used to attach timber, metal, plastic and other materials together. Before selecting any metal fixings, compatibility with adjacent materials should be checked to avoid problems of erosion and appearance. Cheap, unfinished steel fixings will stain some species of timber, especially oak. Use fixings designed for outdoor use such as galvanized, stainless steel, brass or zinc-plated metals.

There are four main methods of connecting metals – mechanical, by fixing bolts, nails, screws and rivets; soldering or brazing, which joins by using a metal or alloy; welding, achieved by pressure or fusion; adhesives, of which the most common are epoxy resins.

Nails are the simplest and cheapest method of fixing timber, plastic and other easily penetrated material together. The holding power will be determined by diameter, length, shape and surface finish. If the nails are to be seen, then the shape and size of the head will be important. Steel nails will stain some species of hardwood. Nails should penetrate the fixing member as deep as possible without splitting it. Round wire nails are the cheapest. Their large heads are unattractive and they are best used where they will not be seen. Annular ring shank nails have slightly protruding rings that create a better grip and are used where strong fixings are required. Lost head nails and panel pins can be used to attach lightweight material to surfaces almost invisibly, but the thinner material can break loose over time. Masonry nails provide a quick fixing into softer masonry, but can cause dense render to shatter.

Screws will make a much stronger connection and can be used to attach timber and soft metals. Wood screws have a length of smooth shank just below the head, which produces a strong cramping effect. Screws that are fully threaded along their length are better for fixing thinner boards, such as fencing. Twin-threaded screws are especially useful for attaching deck boards, when they should be at least double the thickness of the board and ideally penetrate the thickness of the second piece of wood. Pilot holes will be required in hard and damp wood and where splitting might be a problem. Slotted, Phillips and Pozidrive® heads are available as well as some newer versions designed to require less force, making them less susceptible to loosing the screwdriver location point, especially when using an electric screwdriver or drill. Screw heads vary in shape and appearance and some may require counter-sinking. Large bolt-like screws are known as Lag bolts. They pass through a pre-drilled hole and are screwed into the second piece of wood. A washer is usually used under the hexagonal head. Plastic plugs are required to form a strong hold into masonry.

Machine bolts and carriage bolts pass all the way through timber or metal and are fixed with a nut, which is tightened along a threaded end section. Washers are required at both ends of machine bolts, but at only at the nut end of carriage bolts which have a square length of shaft under the head which buries itself into the timber as the nut is tightened. Carriage bolts have a much neater appearance. Bolts should be about 25mm(1in) longer than the combined thickness of the pieces to be bolted together. Stronger and more rigid joints are achieved by using several small bolts rather than a single big one.

Wall anchor bolts are used to attach timber or metal to masonry. A hole (typically 10mm) is drilled into the masonry and through the piece to be connected so that the bolt is passed through and into the hole in the wall. Expanding wall bolts expand as they are tightened so that the body grips the masonry and forms a secure fixing. They are not suitable for use in delicate masonry or close to edges. In this situation an adhesive fixing is better.

Plate fixings, joist hangers, deck fasteners, nail plates, angles, slotted fixing plates, deck clips, and other simple methods of attaching timber and metal together, are now widely available, making some types of construction quick and simple. Some fixings, however, might be difficult to remove, as might be necessary for maintenance purposes or to replace a decayed timber.

Adhesives

Some materials should be joined using adhesives. Securing bolts, metal railings and other components into fragile stone or masonry or close to the edges of walls or surfaces is best achieved with an epoxy-based adhesive, which sets rock hard.

Outdoor adhesives for fixing decking components together are also available with an additional advantage that they expand slightly on contact with damp surfaces to fill slight gaps. Adhesives are specialist items and their success is based upon selecting the correct formula for the application. Modern adhesives are extremely strong and, if used correctly, should form a good and permanent bond outdoors. Use a synthetic resin adhesive or a two-part epoxy resin (both of which have gap-filling capabilities) for outdoor areas which are subject to damp.

Cracks and small gaps can be filled using **exterior grade fillers,** which are formulated to withstand some natural movement.

Glass and Mirror

Glass screens allow visibility and light to pass between separate parts of a garden, whilst still serving as a barrier. Outdoor glass is vulnerable, however, especially if not surrounded by a frame, without which it could easily be missed. If it breaks it is hazardous and may be costly to replace, so in all but the simplest situations (glass houses), glass should be laminated or tempered.

Sheet glass or flat glass can be mirrored, strengthened, tinted, stained and painted to provide a wealth of opportunities for garden applications. It can also be patterned, etched, pressed, embossed or sandblasted to provide further opportunities for commission and invention. The most important consideration will be how the glass is fixed, which will usually require specialist advice.

Glass blocks can be used in the same way as other masonry units. Views through glass blocks are obscure and so some privacy can be maintained, whilst allowing light to pass through. Blocks require special mortar/mastic to hold them together, but work like bricks.

Mirror The quality of the mirrored glass is unimportant, old glass mirrors often being more convincing than newer ones. Use a gate or grille in front of the mirror to discourage birds from attempting to fly through. Make sure the outside edge of the mirror is seale to prevent water seeping in.

Plastics

The use of plastic and plastic products is becoming more common in gardens as manufacturers produce off-the-peg systems for decking, fencing, shades and pergolas, play equipment, furniture and other increasingly clever applications. Many use recycled plastics and make bold claims about sustainability and environmental responsibility, most of which are dubious. The beauty of plastic is most definitely 'in the eye of the beholder', but plastics tend to be cheap, corrosion-resistant, heat-resistant, lightweight and maintenance-free. Designers exploring Perspex and other plastics are looking at the ways in which their integral colour, ability to be shaped, welded, and to transmit light can be exploited.

Perspex (and other similar) is one of the most versatile of materials. A trade name for acrylic sheet material, it is a type of plastic available in a vast range of colours, sheet sizes and thicknesses. Perspex can be clear, translucent or solid, drilled, cut, bent and glued. Sheets can be chamfered to give them a more finished appearance, and they need to be secured to a strong framework to prevent them being blown away. Perspex can also be curved by being heated and bent round a wooden mould, then allowed to cool. Thermal expansion may be expected. The darker coloured sheets absorb more heat and therefore expand slightly in strong sunlight, so an allowance of 0.5 per cent or 5mm($\frac{1}{5}$in) per metre(yard) should be made, especially if one wall panel is placed next to another. Mirrored Perspex is also available.

Perspex stands up well to UK weather conditions, and should keep its colour for at least ten years, with virtually no maintenance.

Geotextiles

These are woven fabrics and felts that are used as weed barriers and filter membranes, to protect slopes from erosion and to reinforce soil against wear and collapse.

They are extremely cheap and make a valuable addition under paving where they can separate layers and prevent material being lost into the subsoil. A geotextile filter placed behind a timber retaining wall will allow water to pass through, but not soil. On the ground such filters allow rainwater to penetrate the soil, but prevent weed growth.

Topsoil

Top soilis a complex balance of highly variable living and dead material. Soil itself is an all-encompassing term for a growing medium that has different layers or horizons. Subsoil is mostly mineral in content, whereas topsoil has higher proportions of organic material with concentrated nutrients to promote plant life. Although the depth of topsoil can vary from a few centimetres to more than 1m(3ft3in), the usual specified depth is about 300mm(1ft). For stability and water supply, adequate topsoil is needed if deeper roots of trees or shrubs are specified.

When importing topsoil it is usual to aim for a texture suited to the location and the proposed planting – this can vary from a lighter soil, such as a sandy loam, to a heavier loam. Avoid clay as in extreme cases dense clay pans can form, preventing drainage.

Topsoil does not need to be extremely fertile, as fertilizer or manure can be added afterwards, but lack of fertility may mean that the topsoil has been poorly stored; topsoils need air to remain healthy and soils that have been piled too high (greater than 2–3m (6–10ft), or stored for over six months, will inevitably begin to degenerate, the structure collapsing and organic matter decomposing in anaerobic conditions.

Recently a broader range of manufactured topsoils has become available, usually as a result of blending subsoils with various bulky organic materials, such as green compost.

Soil pH also needs to be considered. Normally the pH of garden soils lies between the range of 4.5 (acid) and 8.0.

Soil must be free from contamination, which can occur if it has been taken from development sites previously used for factories or industries. Soil must also be free from weeds (a fairly futile aim) and it is more sensible to specify that the soil be free of visible roots from aggressive perennials, such as couch grass or bindweed.

The simplest approach is to refer to the British Standard (BS 3882:1994), which focuses on soil performance. If in the USA, refer to the American Society of Testing and Materials (ASTM) Soil and Rock, Building Stones, Geotextiles Vol. 04.08.

Ordering topsoil

Try to build up a good relationship with your supplier by visiting his premises, finding out what grades are available, checking to see if it stored correctly, asking if he collects from other sites and whether he can deliver direct.

Ask for a sample of soil and check this against the delivery BEFORE it is tipped.

Check the quantity being delivered; if sold by weight, the delivery truck should have a printout; if sold by volume, measure the volume of the delivery truck.

Wall and screen coverings

There are many ways to enhance walls, screens or other built features. The following techniques are some or the principal treatments. With the exception of oil stucco, all these techniques are lime-based.

Sgraffito This technique involves putting down a dark coat of lime mortar followed by a lighter topcoat, which is then carved to reveal the darker coat beneath. Because of their clarity, sgraffito designs can be read from

a distance, the nature of the material also making them durable against the elements.

Oil stucco is fine stucco that can be used for delicate sgraffitto work or for embossed designs. It can also be burnished to a high finish. Lacking the impermeability of lime, it is inappropriate for use on old walls but suitable for contemporary settings where glass, cement and ceramics are used. Completely impervious to water, oil stucco can be incorporated into water features and into urban environments. It can be applied straight on to a gypsum skim, or even on to lightly abraded glass and metal surfaces.

Fresco is an extraordinary technique unchanged for centuries, in which large paintings are made up in daily sections. Two coats of mortar are applied to each section and the image is swiftly applied to the topcoat as it cures, so that a series of transparent glazes are built up and trapped in the surface, so designers must work quickly. and the designs must be meticulously prepared and transferred to the wall before painting begins as there is little margin for error. The beauty of their stony surface and the transparency of their colours are suitable for abstract designs and pure colour and can be used in a number of different ways.

Ceramics Large or small ceramic murals can be applied to most vertical surfaces. These are usually made from high-fired stoneware clay that is robust and frost-proof, and can include a variety of media (paint, ceramics, glass), or might incorporate natural materials, such as slate, marble, granite and pebbles, to achieve the effect.

The design can be impressed on to a large sheet of clay and, once fired, applied to a surface and fixed with an epoxy resin.

BIBLIOGRAPHY

Nearly all of the books listed provide specific further information on the garden elements covered in this book, but a small number are included because they have proved useful and inspirational to the authors.

Agate, E. *Fencing*, British Trust for Conservation Volunteers (BTCV), 1988

Agate, E. *Footpaths*, British Trust for Conservation Volunteers (BTCV), 1996

Agate, E. & Brooks, A. *Dry Stone Walls*, British Trust for Conservation Volunteers (BTCV),1986

American Horticultural Society *Paths and Paving*, Dorling Kindersley, 1999

Anderson, J. and Shiers, D. *The Green Guide to Specification*, Blackwell Science, 2002

Archer-Wills, A. *The Water Gardener*, Frances Lincoln Ltd, 2000

Aurand, C.D. *Fountains and Pools: Construction Guidelines and Specification,* Van Nostrand Reinhold, 1991

Blanc, Alan *Landscape Construction and Detailing,* McGraw Hill Education, 1996

Bradley Hole, C. *The Minimalist Garden,* Mitchell Beazley, 1999

Brookes, J. *John Brookes' Garden Design Book,* Dorling Kindersley, 1991

Brown, J. *The Modern Garden,* Thames and Hudson, 2001

Brown, J. *In Pursuit of Paradise,* HarperCollins, 2004

Conran, T. and Pearson, D. *The Essential Garden Book,* Conran Octopus, 1998

Crowe, Sylvia *Garden Design;* Packard Publishing Ltd, 1981

Fortlage, C. and Phillips, E. *Landscape Construction: Walls, Fences and Railings* Vol. I, Gower,1991

Fortlage, C. and Phillips, E. *Landscape Construction: Roads, Paving and Drainage* Vol. II, Ashgate, 1996

Fortlage, C. and Phillips, E. *Landscape Construction: Earth and Water Retaining Structures* Vol. III, Ashgate, 2001

Fortlage, C. and Phillips, E. *Landscape Construction: Materials, Steps, Ramps and Light Strutures* Vol. IV, Ashgate, 2001

Fox, A. & Murrell, R. *Green Design: A guide to the environmental impact of building materials,* Architectural design and technical press, 1989

Harris, C. and Dines, N. *Timesaver Standards for Landscape Architects,* McGraw-Hill Education, 1998

Dines, N. and Brown, K. *Site Construction Details Manual: TSS,* McGraw-Hill Education, 1998

Hobhouse, P. *The Story of Gardening,* Dorling Kindersley, 2004

Howarth, M. *Pebble Mosaics: Creative designs and techniques for paths, patios and walls,* Search Press Ltd, 1994

Hunningher, E. (ed) *Making Gardens,* Cassell and Co., 2001

Pinder, A. and Pinder, A. *Beasley's Design and Detail of the Space about Buildings,* Spon 1991

Raine, J. *Garden Lighting,* Hamlyn, 2001

Stevens, D., Huntington, L. and Key, R. *The Complete Book of Garden Design, Construction and Planting,* Cassell and Co., 1994

Stevens, D. *The Garden Design Sourcebook: The essential guide to garden materials and structures,* Conran Octopus, 1998

Fences and Gates, Sunset Books, 1996

Decks, Sunset Books, 1996

Symes, M. (ed) *Fountains: Splash and spectacle,* Thames and Hudson, 1998

Wiles, R. *RHS Guide to Garden Structures,* Mitchell Beazley, 1992

Waymark, J. *Modern Garden Design,* Thames and Hudson, 2003

Garden Design Journals, *Landscape Design Trust,* Burlington Press

AUTHORS' ACKNOWLEDGEMENTS

Our main thanks go to Pippa Rubinstein and Judith Robertson at R & R Publishing for their belief in this book, skill in putting it together and their patience in fitting around our busy lives. Also to Tim Dann, responsible for interpreting and developing Richard's sketch illustrations.

Our thanks also to Rochelle Greayer who checked that the text complied with American conventions, and converted UK terms and measurements. Both Amanda Crabbe at The English Gardening School, and in the early stages, John Blake, have also been very supportive.

Rosemary Alexander thanks

For my part, this book is the result of years of working and teaching in the landscape and garden design business. I should like to thank Brian Clouston and Partners, from whom I learnt so much in my early years; Anthony Du Gard Pasley, who revolutionized the way I looked at design and planting, and all my colleagues, fellow tutors and students at The English Gardening School, from whom I still learn so much.

Richard Sneesby thanks

I should also like to thank a few people who have helped organize my thoughts on the subject and given valuable advice during the writing of this book. In particular Gerry Metcalf, the best design teacher I know, Mark Cowell and Mike Westley, all three of whom are amazingly knowledgeable and constantly inspirational. Owen Manning was the first person I met who explained why landscape construction and detailing was so crucial to good design. James Wilson and I taught jointly for much of the 1990s and together developed a method of teaching landscape and garden detailing which is revealed in this book. Also my parents, Pat and Norman Sneesby, for encouraging me to work with the landscape. My main thanks, however, must go to my wife Henrietta who is amazingly patient, always greatly improves my crude ideas and is a constant friend. Without her I would have had no time to put this book together.

INDEX